Goddess Powered

ENTREPRENEUR

Aligning your business with your soul

AUTHORS:

Ceryn Rowntree, Deanna Thomas, Iona Russell,
Jasmin Baljak, Karishma Sharma, Miriam Husby Stener,
Rachel Watson, Tierra Womack MBA, Wendy Dixon,
Yolandi Boshoff, Michelle Maslin-Taylor,
Tanja Stephanie Rug, Rachel Smithbone

BALBOA.PRESS
A DIVISION OF HAY HOUSE

Balboa Press books may be ordered through booksellers or by contacting:

Balboa Press
A Division of Hay House
1663 Liberty Drive
Bloomington, IN 47403
www.balboapress.co.uk
UK TFN: 0800 0148647 (Toll Free inside the UK)
UK Local: (02) 0369 56325 (+44 20 3695 6325 from outside the UK)

Print information available on the last page.

ISBN: 978-1-9822-8512-8 (sc)
ISBN: 978-1-9822-8513-5 (e)

Balboa Press rev. date: 01/27/2022

Introduction

Welcome to Goddess Powered Entrepreneur!

The inspiration behind this project came from my own experience as an entrepreneur. Having been a spiritual entrepreneur for almost eight years I wanted to reinforce an important message that often gets lost in the online noise.

We can feel pulled to have the perfect website, have the perfect landing page, have a podcast, have a lead magnet, have followers, have likes – sometimes the striving takes us down a path that brings resistant, struggle, comparison, and a downright sense of having all of the joy zapped out of your brilliant soul-led business idea!!!

The message that is often forgotten - **Your soul knows.**

Within the pages of this book, you will learn and be inspired by 13 incredible soul-led entrepreneurs who are tuning into their soul's purpose, allowing their journey as an entrepreneur to be a one of flow, alignment, and heart connection.

As we shift into a new world and way of being we are being pulled towards integrity, authenticity, and soul connection, and this is a powerful combination when applied to your own business and day to day business interactions and communication.

Do not be afraid of going against the norm, instead tune into your inner Goddess and let her take your business on a magnificent journey, touching and impacting the hearts of many around the world.

My wish for you is that by the time you complete this book you are reconnected to and reminded of that beautiful spark you felt when you made the courageous decision to become an entrepreneur, you have a clear vision, your mission and passion grow, your confidence shines through, and you shift into allowing your soul-led business to flow in a perfectly aligned way, filled with joy, connection, and prosperity!

Tons of Love

Leanne x
Founder – She Speaks Media & She Speaks Talk Radio

Soul messages from the co-authors

"I am passionate about the power of conscious entrepreneurship to change the world. When business is soul powered, guided by source and heart, magic is birthed, and this world needs more magic. As individuals, being a sacred business owner offers the space and container for massive growth and the incredible opportunity to create our lives exactly as we desire them to be. This stuff matters folks." – Rachel Smithbone

"To be a soul creator whose business is based on God/Source working through me to help create spiritual wealth in partnership with God/source is the highest and most sacred honour, to inspire other entrepreneurs, businesses, world leaders to open themselves up to possibilities of what their God given potential is and to bring global change, one spark at a time, to create a world of god/source/illuminated entrepreneurship is the dream" – Jasmin Baljak

"Age is not a barrier to creating our dreams and living our true-life purpose. I stopped myself from achieving my dreams for many years; however, by trusting my intuition I moved to the other end of the country setting up Intuitive Life with Wendy Dixon and am now living the life I was always meant to live. With my Intuitive Life Coaching Programme, and 1-2-1 life / business readings, I support midlifers to identify and live their life purpose with joy and passion. By using my intuition, I am able to ensure my programmes are specifically aligned to the individual, helping to identify blocks, gain clarity in moving life forward, and guidance in working towards achieving those dreams. Reviewing next steps in business and / or personal life give a clearer vision of the future, to move life forward in a positive and focussed manner" - Wendy Dixon

"There is no blueprint for entrepreneurship and everyone's definition of success is unique to them. When you are first starting out as an entrepreneur, you can be inundated with the noise of "to-do's" you're told MUST be done to have a dream business. And you may even feel as though you're a bit intimidated by the thought of having a highly successful business with many moving parts if you ALREADY feel overwhelmed. However, I strongly believe that success CAN be simple, enjoyable and full of the time freedom you desire if you have the right mindset, foundation & systems in place. My hope is as you read the pages of this book, you find inspiration to define success on your terms, fully believing that it is possible!" – Tierra Womack MBA

"Look at you go! Forging your own path as an entrepreneur is brave and beautiful and oh, so challenging! You are an epic human being. The words in this book are here to lift and guide you. Store up in your heart the words that feel good and true for you right now. Come back later to uncover new wisdom. Leave behind what doesn't make your soul sing. We are all here, rooting for you to be your own guiding star." – Rachel Watson

"The journey of Entrepreneurship is one of the most transformative paths you could ever walk. Each little step that you take is calling a part of who you are back to you. This can be hard, and we have to learn to trust ourselves, listen to ourselves and take responsibility for all our choices. But that is really the best part, because there will be a moment when you feel that flow, when you hear your Soul and it will all be worth it. That moment when you remember who you are." – Yolandi Boshoff

"Doing the work that feels like your life and Soul's purpose is an incredible thing - as a Therapist, Coach and professional Medium I know that first hand. But entrepreneurship can be lonely work too, and it is so important to know that you aren't alone in this. My hope for this project is that you remember not only the power of yourself and your own work, but of the connections that are available to support you on this path of doing the work you are called to, and take you ever closer to your own place of true fulfillment in your work and life." – Ceryn Rowntree

"As I see the smiles and joy that my mission brings, where I get to help women to activate deeper levels of success, happiness, fun, freedom, fabulousness, love and so much more - it makes it all worth it. Each one of us has a reason of why we were put on this planet and Entrepreneurship with a fun magical twist is part of my reason. What is your mission for your Spiritual Entrepreneurial journey? That vision you have IS possible. You are a powerful, limitless, creator and YOU get to decide what energy, vibe, uniqueness you bring to the Entrepreneurial world. Know that you are never alone on this journey. Let me see you rise sister! " – Karishma Sharma

Contents

Chapter One

CERYN ROWNTREE

Why going it alone does not have to be lonely

An hour on Instagram and you are likely to think that working for yourself is THE most fun and interesting thing you can do.

All those #girlbosses looking perfectly coiffed and drinking coffee in their picture perfect kitchens; the #solopreneurs having the time of their lives as they work from a laptop on the beach; and the #soulpreneurs in my own industry, talking about the many benefits that working for themselves has brought.

Of course there is much truth in that; working for ourselves, doing the things that bring us meaning, is an incredible thing, never more so when it also means we can build a life that we love on the schedule that works for us. There is no denying that going it alone in business can bring many benefits to us and our lives.

But there is something important I want us to remember; something I wish that I and many friends and clients had known up front – that going it alone does not have to mean being lonely.

I made the transition into self-employment after fifteen years in the corporate world. I was used to a buzz of constant meetings, chats with colleagues in the office when a change in perspective was needed, and lunch or coffee breaks with friends who could always be relied upon on the days when I just needed to step away and remember what was important in life. It was busy and incredibly stressful, but it was definitely never quiet!

Then I began working for myself full-time and things…well, changed. Suddenly I was working from home alone all day; and while I talked to clients throughout the day, they were not the people to bounce ideas off, offload my worries to, or talk things through with, so I could hear a different perspective.

And while I knew it may take a bit of getting used to, even suspected that it may get a little lonely from time to time, I was not prepared for just how much that might impact my creativity, motivation or the anxious thoughts that began to whiz around my mind with no one to give me an outside perspective.

It took me to a point where I was unsure how to move forward, and even worse than that I found myself wondering if it was even the right thing *for* me to move forward. All the passion that had carried me out of my old job and into the work I passionately believed in seemed to have been swept away, leaving me with an uninspired brain that felt empty apart from the little inner voice that seemed to have become my most regular workmate, and wanted nothing more than for me to stop shining my light and instead shrink back into myself.

Of course, I have also heard of people who have gone completely the other way; those whose egos – once left untended – grew out of control and had them racing ahead to deliver things they had initially intended for a year or two down the line even as they were still trying to work out the very basics of their business.

And other people too; those who have gone into business with the best of intentions to help people, but without the right personal support to keep themselves safe and grounded, ended up projecting a lot of their own inner struggles onto the clients they were working with.

For me, this need for interpersonal support and the risks that come without it, is one of the most significant emotional and mental challenges those of us working for ourselves must be mindful of – particularly in the early days of our business. It is why I passionately believe it is important for us to build up the kind of support networks that can support us through whatever challenges we face when working for ourselves.

Some of the greatest support I have had has been from friends who were in a similar position; those who were a step or two ahead of me on their own journey and knew just how tough it could be, but also the benefits that lie on the other side of every challenge each of us face.

But I also know that not all of us have friends in the same position; I have spoken to many clients over the years who are the only ones in their families or friendship groups to ever go out on their own and pursue their passion as a business. They have found themselves feeling even lonelier still when no one understood what they were doing enough to offer genuine support.

Even in those cases though, there is never a need for any of us to go through the experience of building or sustaining a business alone. Nor is there a need for us to suffer in silence through those early days that are often, even for the most successful businesses and most resilient women – tough and uncertain.

Which is where those professional support opportunities can really come into their own.

Things like networking groups, that not only help us remember we are not alone, but also give us a safe space to talk through our challenges, work out our ideas and share our experiences. Or co-working groups that allow us to work alongside one or more entrepreneurs – either in person or online – reducing the risk of us experiencing the loneliness that comes when we find ourselves working alone.

Maybe you would benefit from bringing Mentor on board; to hold that safe, supportive, and confidential space that helps you keep going on your own terms. Without feeling that this is a journey you are taking alone; or a coach whose role is to help you continue moving forwards, overcoming any obstacles in your path, and growing and developing in the way that feels right for you and your business.

Whichever option – or options – you prefer, the important thing to remember is that there *are* options. In fact at times, it can seem as though there are too many options, leaving your head in a whirl over which you should choose! And that no matter how lonely the life of an entrepreneur can feel, there are always people and groups out there to support you.

With all that in mind, how do you even start to consider the kind of support you are looking for? How do you find something that fits?

For me it begins with good, old fashioned research, the kind that has you turning inwards long before you look at what anyone else may or may not offer. Take some time away from your desk, maybe take a walk in nature or sit in meditation – as you consider the following:

- What are your challenges at the moment?

  Try to be reasonably generic with this. Do not get too bogged down in specifics. Instead, consider more general ideas like time-management, loneliness, motivation.

- What is your current support network like, both in terms of people and the support they can and do offer?

  If it helps to consider this visually, grab a piece of paper and a pen, drawing the people closest to you personally and professionally – that is something you can definitely carry forward to the next question…

- What do you feel like you are missing in terms of your support network?

  Is there a particular subject you need help with, a particular challenge you could do with more support on, or a more specific requirement that you know would help you?

- What sort of people would you like to support you on this journey?

The psychologist Carl Jung once said that who we are tends to be shaped by the six people we spend the most time with. That is a line I think about a lot whenever I am looking to welcome new people into my life and my work; are they the kind of people I want to be like too?

With many groups and individuals on the market offering countless different options, these questions are a vital way to ensure you are rooted in what you actually need rather than being easily swayed into something that may be good for another person, but is not necessarily the right fit for you or your business.

From there, it is time to put your request out there into the Universe. There are many ways to do this; as a practising witch, my favourite time is always around the New Moon. This is a ritual that I use, try it for yourself.

Take a piece of paper and write your request out as an affirmative statement along the lines of:

> "I have found and am working with the perfect mentor for my business who is supportive and discerning, and can help me work through my many ideas to find the right path forwards."

On the night of the New Moon put the paper under a glass or bottle of water, ideally on a windowsill or elsewhere in the light of the Moon, for two or three hours (or even for 24 hours if you would prefer – a full day of lunar light is never a bad thing for a ritual!).

Once you are ready head outside and hold your water up to the Moon so that you can see the Moon – or the sky if it is too cloudy – through the water then read out your affirmation three times.

Finally drink the water, and as it flows into your system imagine your request being granted and the perfect person or group coming into your life.

Once you have decided what you want and the offers and suggestions have begun flowing your way, how do you choose which one is right for you?

My own experiences, both good and bad, and those of the clients I have worked with over the years, have taught me that it comes down to three pretty important things:

- You truly believe this person or group has your best interests at heart. Whether money changes hands or not, this feels like a supportive space in which you could and would be supported to grow.
- You leave each session feeling lighter and inspired. You may feel scared and even a little tired, as you have processed some of your challenges or been called out on some of the ways you were keeping yourself small, it always feels expansive rather than restrictive.
- It just feels right. Yup, it comes back to good old gut instinct. As entrepreneurs, we know how important it is to pay attention to the feelings, physical and emotional, that arise within us in relation to particular situations. Be sure to trust your gut with this one, for the sake of you and your business.

Remember that seeking support as an entrepreneur never means you have failed or are in some way struggling; often it is exactly the opposite! Instead, this is about valuing your business and its need for support, but more to the point it is about valuing yourself. Remember that you do not have to do everything alone. There are always people out there willing and able to support your growth and cheer you on. Not just from the side-lines, but right beside you too.

Chapter Two

DEANNA THOMAS

Trust the timing of your life.

It can be exhausting work being a business owner, but being a spiritual entrepreneur comes with its own unique set of challenges. Still, it is one of the most rewarding and life-changing things that you can do.

My name is Deanna, and I am a Spiritual Entrepreneur; a mum to 3 young children; and I live in the Northeast of the Uk. I am excited to have this opportunity to share my story along with my top tips to help you create a truly aligned business too.

For the past eight years, I have been working to build two different spiritual businesses and aligning my life with my soul's purpose. I was running a spiritual and holistic centre in the Northeast. The events and speakers, and activities I was hosting were incredible. It has been an amazing journey, and I have loved every minute. Alongside that, I am building a well-being business offering readings, energy healing sessions and complementary therapies. I have received several awards over the past couple of years which is lovely because I put my heart and soul into helping other people.

I thought I had my path all figured out, and then the pandemic hit. It has been a challenging period for so many people, and business owners were hit very hard.

Surprisingly, for me, it was a bit of a blessing in disguise, because it helped me revisit my original vision, created and planned three years ago. It allowed me the space and time to check in with my soul and make necessary changes. I had to let go of the things that I no longer felt aligned with, and now I only have one business. But it is truly aligned with who I am and my purpose.

It's funny because one minute you think you have everything figured out and the next, you feel like you don't have a clue. Perhaps that resonates with you; maybe you have been thinking about following your dreams and using your intuition to create a business truly aligned with your soul. Maybe you have tried running a business in the past, and it has not worked out the way you had hoped.

Here's the truth; it is normal to have doubts and fears. Whether you have or have not been in this position before. Those doubts are what I call mind monkeys, and we need to put them to one side because if we listened to them every time they spoke, we would never do anything, would we?

I believe there is a reason why you are reading this book, and dear goddess, I am super excited for the journey ahead of you!

If you want to create a business that is aligned with your soul, and all to do with spirituality and wellbeing, then this chapter can help you. Just before you dig in and read the rest of this chapter, let's have a quick check-in:

- Are you prepared to do whatever it takes to make your business come alive?
- Do you have the time and energy to be consistent, show up every day, and put the work in?
- Are you committed to discovering what your soul's purpose is?
- Are you a quitter?

If you can answer yes to these questions, then continue; otherwise, this chapter might not be the one for you right now.

Living a life of purpose

How do you find your purpose? It's a question lots of people ask me.

There was a time where I had no idea what "soul purpose" meant. I did not understand until I discovered who I really was. From then on, I started learning all I could about the law of attraction and spirituality. This helped me find my purpose.

Your purpose is the reason you are here. It is what you are called to do, and it is connected to all the things that light you up. It is those very things that you feel passionate about. If your business is aligned to your soul's purpose, it will be the driving force moving you forward, as it is the very reason you do what you do.

I know that I am running my business from my souls' purpose because it never really feels like I am at work. If you can recognise that in yourself it is a sign that you are on the right track. Everyone has a soul's purpose, it is a deep inner calling within all of us. I believe that we are all on a unique path to find our soul's mission and fulfil our dreams through our soul's purpose.

Diana Ross, a famous singer, said a quote that resonates with me, she said: "You can't just sit there and wait for people to give you that golden dream. You've got to get out there and make it happen yourself." I feel this is so true.

If the people around you are not feeling as excited as you, or are not supportive of your business ideas, try not to get disheartened. They might not understand what your desire to create your own business means to you. That's ok because it's *your* purpose, not theirs.

When I first discovered my soul's purpose, people around me did not understand. They thought it was unrealistic; that I should have a normal job. But that did not light me up. I am so pleased that I stopped listening to their opinions because I would not be doing what I love now.

It is a powerful thing to know your soul's purpose because once you do, you cannot help but inject magic and passion into all of your work. It gives you so much strength and confidence to go forward and create something unique and highly rewarding for you. I feel it is tapping into the magic within you. It will not seem like hard work to get your business off the ground because it will all be exciting. People will be drawn to you by your energy and enthusiasm.

It can be really helpful to journal your ideas and inspirations down, so here are some questions you can use as journal prompts:

- What is your soul's purpose?
- If you could do anything for a business, what would you do?
- What type of spiritual business do you want to have?
- What is your passion?
- Who will you help/work with?
- How will you help them?

You may already have the answers to these questions. If you do, that's great.

This process can also help you check in with your business vision and goals, helping you be sure that you are in alignment with your purpose and on the right track. The clearer you can be on who you help and how you help them, the better your marketing will speak to the clients you want to attract. When it comes to social media and marketing, it is important to build a brand that people can get to know and trust.

Tuning into who you are, and what you do

What problems do you solve for your ideal clients? This is at the core of what you do, and it is a powerful way to become truly aligned with your business and your purpose. This can help you find the best niche for your business.

Finding a niche is a great way to help your business stand out from your competitors. Look at people who do the same as you and see if they have a speciality (niche) and how that comes across.

For example, I am partnered with a high profile essential oils company, and there are lots of people who do what I do. I needed to do something to stand out from the crowd. I am a certified aromatherapist, qualified and insured to deliver meditation classes. I am also an advanced crystal healer. I have incorporated these skills and created a niche for my business. Now I share classes and talks, and deliver meditation sessions, on using crystals with essential oils.

I could be put off by knowing that many other people are doing something similar to me, but all that tells me is that there is a lot of demand for it. It is a huge industry, and it is how I help people that makes the difference.

Here are some questions that you can answer in your journal:

- What niche are you an expert in?
- How can you help people? What problems do you solve?
- What are you passionate about Teaching/ Sharing?

Many spiritual business owners find it hard to separate their spirituality from their business because they are so connected to one another. Your soul purpose will always guide you towards the niche that you have the most knowledge, experience, or passion with. Trust your intuition and see what insights come up for you.

Shining your light

One of the biggest challenges I see many spiritual business owners struggle with is comparison.

Theodore Roosevelt said that "Comparison is the thief of joy."

I really resonate with that quote. Why do we compare ourselves to other people? They can never be you, nor you, them. It is a wonderful thing that each of us is unique. It means no one else can do things the way that you do.

Flowers do not compare their beauty to each other; they just grow and attract the bees and insects that are a perfect match for them. I believe that there is enough room for everyone and an abundance of business and clients for us all. Do not let other people prevent you from shining your light; you just have to do you and let other people be who they are.

When we compare ourselves to other people, we begin to question our worth, and we don't shine as brightly. We become stagnant because we stop growing and keep ourselves stuck. Here's the truth; No one will know what you do unless you tell them, so you have to be showing up and sharing who you are and what you do. Share the magic within you because your purpose is to grow and flourish. In doing so, you help others do the same.

Consistency is key

Your mindset, your habits and your routines are not only the building blocks for success as you work towards your wellness goals; they also form the foundation for your business. Energy flows where your awareness and focus go.

Social media has a huge impact on finding our ideal clients and figuring out how we connect with them. Share your voice and your values in the posts you publish, and they will speak to the people you want to work with.

Consistency on social media is key to building a brand that people will love and trust. I see many people struggling with this. They set up a page, and they post for a little while. Then they get fed up with it because it is not growing as fast as they would like. They stop posting, and that affects the visibility and algorithms of the page, reducing the size of their audience.

Suppose you can spend one day a month focused on scheduling all your social media posts. This will strongly benefit your business. You will help boost the algorithms on your pages, and you will be showing up every day in people's newsfeeds. Canva is a wonderful free tool that you can use to create content, and there are many other applications that can help you schedule posts for Instagram and Facebook. Have a play and find what works for you.

To grow your business, you need to network and develop relationships with people. People buy from people they connect with. Think about where your ideal clients hang out on social media; where can you find them? You can join groups and networks to discover where they are and begin to build relationships with people. Spend a few minutes every day popping into other groups where your ideal clients hang out, commenting on posts, and being of value.

Good luck, enjoy every moment!

Chapter Three

IONA RUSSELL

When Divine inspiration strikes

It is 3am and I have been dancing between insomnia and dead sleep; sleep so deep I cannot get up. It is like I am wearing a weighted chainmail blanket of pure exhaustion.

Have you ever felt that you were riding a rocky rollercoaster; fluctuating between overwhelm and burnout, as you try to force yourself into the old patriarchal business hustle paradigm, when all you want is a business that speaks from your soul and feels easy, abundant, and impactful.

Perhaps you are dreaming of 'one day' in the future starting a business that feels like your soul purpose. But you do not know when or how or what. Or you have so many ideas that you freeze, unsure of WTF to do, trying to figure out what is divine inspiration and what is fear based.

Me too. I have been there, and sometimes I still jump on that rocky rollercoaster. Usually when I am out of alignment in my life, relationships, and business, because they are all connected. We cannot work on one area and neglect the others.

The business of being spiritual, abundant and in alignment is a balancing act. The secret is to let it be joyful, do the Inner work, and be adaptable.

Being adaptable is actually a superpower; if you combine it with divine inspiration, tangible action and heart felt gusto.

Back to my 3am dance of the dead.

I have a fecking epic life and a business I love. I have amazing relationships with my soul family my divine siSTARs and brothers. I have a radio show, and a new one launching. I collaborate on live events "Soul Dancer - Live Your Magic." I have travelled the world and spoken on global stages. Currently, I am making more in my business than I ever have before and selling out events. I have written two solo books and contributed to four collaborations.

I am living the life I always dreamed of living.

So, WTF am I wide awake at 3 am riding that rocky rollercoaster?

Because we all have to start somewhere, and we all battle shadows that we need to heal along the way. We are all a work in progress. There is no right or wrong way to do this. You just do you with an open heart.

How? I hear you ask.

I emigrated back to the UK from living in Texas; with a divorce in hand, a reluctant teenager, my mother's recent death weighing on my heart, and tenants in my house. Technically homeless for 4 months. I realised I had to reinvent myself AGAIN, and went into survival mode to provide for me and my son. Never again would I be reliant on someone else or a bricks and mortar business. I knew in that moment from then on I had to BE my business and I jumped with both feet onto the entrepreneurial train.

This involved getting my VIP ticket stamped with and verified to;

- see opportunities where others do not
- follow divine inspiration
- see challenges as learning, lessons, and blessings
- be open to unexpected and unknown doors opening
- getting support from those further ahead, and listening, watching, and learning from them
- remain heart focused with soul

- do the inner work and heal my own trauma, from this and all lifetimes
- be humble and share my story from love
- dust myself off when I fall, dry my tears, and get back on the train, accept rejection as part of the course and dream of better days ahead
- believe and know that I can flourish, thrive, and feel fulfilled following my Dreams, being authentically me, to reach my purest potential.

It is not always easy. but if it fills your heart with expansion energy when you think about it, and the idea of doing anything else is unimaginable and would feel like your soul is dying. Then you are choosing to live the life you were born to live, and you are embarking on the dance of your souls path.

One of the biggest questions I am asked is 'How do I know if I am on the right path.' The path you are on is the right path. There is no wrong path. You may be taking a detour, in some cases a very long detour. But every path is the right path for you right now. We get to learn from our detours.

Let me ask you; are you going to listen to the shouts from your ego or the whispers of your soul? Because you are here to create heaven on earth with the medicine that is written across your heart. Only you can do this dance and activate others with your divine dance of the soul. This is your purpose, and we need you; I need you; the world needs you to dance and join the epic entrepreneurial train.

What is that jewel, the spark that is within you waiting to dance?

This is what keeps me awake at 3am

- Am I enough?
- Who am I to create this; do this; be this; soul dance?
- How will this work?
- I should go back to 'normal work'?
- All the 'things' of the patriarchal business model that I 'should' be doing
- Am I crazy?

- What will they say? Think? Do?
- Comparison analysis etc

YES! Even those of us who appear to have it all together still have doubts, still lie awake at night, still wonder 'What if?' But this is when I know you and I are not coming from a soul aligned space, we are not following our own unique divine inspiration and have moved from our heart space to our head space aka the penthouse of the body (which is in disconnect with the heart and soul), we have moved from love into fear.

Let's return to love. And return to the dance of our Soul.

We are either living in Fear or Love. When we are not living from a place of love, we are calling for Love. We all have innate wellbeing, health, and happiness within us. We have just forgotten; who we were before "they" told us who to be; before we told ourselves how to be; before we put on the Mask of conformity and hid behind it. We can choose to transform our lives by "rebooting" ourselves to who we are at our core on a Soul level, back to our authentic Self.

Remembering who we are—the wild and gifted wise wo(man), soul siSTAR—a Spiritual being having a human experience. It is time for you to Shine Bright and BE Magnificent!

It is time to finally create the magic that you are here to create with your business. And finish the dance of your souls gifts.

It is time to tune in and listen to the Divine inspiration that can strike when we least expect it. I can share tips. But be ready because once you start to tune in you may get so many ideas that you do not know where to begin. You may feel overwhelmed.

BREATHE and feel into these ideas; you will feel in your heart if this is a true inspiration. Trust these thoughts, trust yourself, and be open to inspiration when you least expect it. In the shower, or driving. Anywhere! It jumps out into your awareness and is totally unrelated to what you are doing at the time.

Find your tribe

Open your heart, listen to the conversations you are having and take action. Divine inspired action. Without action there can be no reaction and creation.

You can choose who aligns with your soul mission and matches your vibration. I suggest getting clear on a few key areas around your mission and coming back to these before you say yes to everything. Only say yes to what feels good within your soul.

- How are you showing up in your life?
- What is being mirrored back to you?

We get to choose how we show up, and how we co-create our reality.

The new paradigm of entrepreneurship is collaboration. No hierarchy. Women sitting in circle metaphorically, physically, and spiritually supporting each other. Together we rise.

Today I invite you to pause and contemplate. There is inspiration in the pause.

It is the space where the magic gets in. In the same way that music is not made up of the sounds of the notes, but of the spaces between the notes. A single note is just a sound. A collection of notes playing together with varying spaces is a piece of music and inspiration.

I digress.... You want to know HOW.

Let's begin with some journal prompts;

- What do you need to do to create the life you want?
- Where do you want to be in twelve months?
- What are the steps to get there?
- Are you willing to do them? If not, let this go.

It is that simple.

For example, I have never had a six-pack, and I never will. Not because I cannot, but because I am not willing to put in the time and effort to get there. That is one less thing for me to worry about. No point beating myself up about it. I am not staying stuck in a cycle of "woe is me" about my lack of a six-pack. I choose not to do this, so I can move on and focus on what I *am* willing to do.

What do YOU choose to change or let go of? BE honest with yourself

> *It's not who you are that holds you back;*
> *it's who you THINK you are not that holds you back!"*
> Denis Waitley

Too many people are trying to fit into the box. You get to break out of the box and break FREE! If you do not feel that your business is aligned to who you want to be and how you want to be contributing to the world then try these questions;

- Who are you surrounding yourself with?
- What do you spend time googling?
- What is your mission?
- What is the one thing that is missing in your business?
- What is the magic you want to birth into this world?
- If you had to redesign your personality, what three qualities would you KEEP? Write them down.

You are Everything!

Everything you need—courage, strength, compassion, love—is already within you.

Everything you seek is within you already.

Everything you need is right there inside you.

You were born amazing, confident, and perfect, but along the way, you have forgotten that.

Sometimes, we forget it was ever there.

Sometimes, we doubt ourselves.

We look for "it" outside of us.

We look for validation and acceptance externally.

Stop! Pause!

You can reset yourself, just like a factory restore of your own internal self—back to You!

You are Amazing!

You were born knowing you are Magnificent, Confident, Courageous, Compassionate, Loved, Perfect and knowing that the Possibilities for you are Limitless.

This knowing is still there within you!

Do you remember?

Do You remember how Amazing You Are?

You are Magnificent,

You are Confident,

You are Courageous,

You are Compassionate,

You are Loved,

You are Perfect...

...and the Possibilities are Limitless

Try this 'Peaceful Practice'

- Set a timer for two minutes
- Without overthinking it, make a list of all your accomplishments.
- Look to celebrate you and look to see the common thread, the lesson learnt, the obstacles overcome, the impact you have had already.

Your gifts are hidden in plain sight, you do not need to go searching outside yourself. Look within. Trust your heart.

Take inspired action and know that you are a divine gift to this world with your own magic.

Now go live your life and remember to always.

Return to Love.

Choose Your Tribe.

Return to your soul mission and feel into and BE open to Divine inspiration.

And listen to the whispers of your soul.

You too can rise up, up level, and live your purest potential.

Chapter Four

JASMIN BALJAK

Source and Entrepreneurship

To be an entrepreneur is to have grit, determination, an unstoppable mindset and to be connected to Source.

This connection takes you to the zone, into the flow state where you work in a partnership with your higher power, a collaboration between the spiritual mind and your body.

You may ask how you combine Source with being an entrepreneur.

Let's expand on what Source is.

> *"Your Source can be God, the Tao, Divine mind, Krishna or whatever else you call your higher power"* – Wayne Dyer

For the purpose of this chapter, we will talk about Source.

Source is a combination of Spirit and Creative Energy, it is all visible things, thus all invisible life and intelligence. It is Spirit, Love, Wisdom and Intelligence, and Power. It is Omnipotence (all-knowing), Omniscience (all knowledge), and Omnipresence (everywhere).

Just for a second, imagine tapping into your higher power every day, communicating consistently, and trusting the daily whispers of what is being said to you. Knowing an invisible intelligence is always softly talking to you, guiding you and providing answers. For me it may be a simple request to leave what I am doing, go to the shop and do something that I was not planning that day; it is always saying "yes" to the whispers because Source knows best, maybe even knows better! Tuning into these daily hints and trusting them will lead to you trusting more and more and help you form a partnership with your higher power.

I believe in working with Source; in trusting and getting into a daily flow of not working out the destination nor the answers by being in "flow" and enjoying the journey. Source will work out the rest. If you tap into Source daily through dedicated prayer, listening to what is being asked of you and only answering yes, I promise that whatever you need will be provided to you and more, even more than you could have ever dreamed.

> *No prayer, no power. Some Prayer some Power. Great Prayer, great power.*

For me, being an Entrepreneur of Wealth, and coaching World Leaders, happened after I began attending Spiritual School on my path to becoming a Billionaire Entrepreneur. When I first started studying to become a Spiritual Practitioner and attending business school, I discovered that the two go hand in hand.

Within the first lesson, my teacher asked the class "Who wants to be a millionaire?" Most of the class raised their hands, but I thought, "That's not what I want." I already had had a great career and made very good money, so I did not raise my hand. But then she asked, "Who wants to be a billionaire?"

This got my attention! I thought "I have always wanted this. Could I be this?" No one claimed it, so she asked again. Still, I hesitated. "One of you must want this" she said as if she knew. Next minute I heard myself saying "ME" and put my hand up. "Good," she said, "One of you has claimed it!".

Fast forward and 6 months later, my world is a blur. I am now a published author, I speak on Radio, I am writing my part in a TV Show, I have more books being published, and I speak to international audiences.

I know that Source is working with me, a natural synergy to reach Billionaire Mountain, I call this Mount Kilimanjaro.

How did this all happen?

They say that when you truly look for your tribe you find them. I have always wanted to find my tribe; my people, women and men who are spiritual and who inspire one another. Every successful Entrepreneur has a tribe of support people, coaches, mentors, friends, and people who get them!

I want to share how to be in Source. Source Energy is where the magic happens for me and you, being in Spiritual "Light" and finding who you are meant to be as an entrepreneur:

On rising, I start my day as Wayne Dyer taught me. Before my feet hit the ground, with gratitude. I say: thank you, thank you, thank you (3 times) for what the new day brings.

I work on 5 minutes of journaling; this teaches me how to recognise JOY and remember each day what makes me happy. Joy is infectious and increases exponentially. Keeping a journal will show you what makes you happy and remind you of what you need to do to create even more joy. You cannot manifest or reach a flow state without being in a joy state.

I listen to the silence of the day before the sun rises. I am finding that I can hear across greater distances, hear more birdsong, hear traffic from many, many, miles away. If you listen carefully, the earth has a heartbeat, energy. If you listen carefully enough it hums; this excites me.

I read 5-10 minutes of a spiritual book that inspires me or a writer I like. I am currently reading Rebecca Campbell, Light is the New Black, an amazing writer.

I then do "Affirmative Prayer" and ask Source to work with me on whatever I need. It could be I need help with sales and marketing; whatever is needed as an entrepreneur. Note: when doing affirmative prayer, get into a joyful state and declare what is your intention at a feeling rate of 2000%

Then I dance for 5 minutes, as Sonia Choquette showed me; as a wild, divine, crazy, feminine Goddess – for 5 minutes. Dance baby! Like no one is watching and laugh.

Then my Mirror Work, just like Louise Hays taught me. Looking into my Golden handheld mirror: I say I love you; I really, really, love you (thank you, LuLu).

Next: Exercise, whether it is a brisk walk near water, a dive into the ocean, Bootcamp, whatever makes me feel alive – even 10 minutes of exercise releases serotonin (the feel-good hormone).

Grounding mat: when working indoors, or when I do not have the opportunity to touch grass, I use a grounding mat for my feet.

For a minimum of 30 minutes a day, you must indulge in being creative i.e., painting, a walk in nature, baking, whatever brings you "joy" – joy is the magic elixir of life.

Lastly: I want you to get into conversation with Source. First, you must learn to sit still and do nothing for 5 minutes a day. Here; do not talk, just take a deep breath in and breath out and a deeper breath and breath out and then start a conversation with Source. Something as simple as "Good morning, here I am."

Slowly, slowly my brothers and sisters you will start to hear the whispers of Source telling you what to do next. This is how you form a strong entrepreneurial partnership with your higher power.

Being an entrepreneur involves:

- Getting into a daily spiritual practice
- Being in Joy (essential)
- Building that relationship with Source
- Surrounding yourself with a team of coaches (a Business Coach, Leadership Coach, Strategic Coach etc).
- Finding a Brand and Marketing Expert to create a brand for you, colours, fonts; creating a professional presence.
- Learning to understand sales and marketing; become an expert.
- Be Omni-present as Alan Lazar advised.

   Being omnipresent is being on every platform you can think of. Radio and TV. Becoming an author will earn you respectability.

Social media; if you are posting on Facebook post on Instagram too, people love consistency. Post daily, get recording on Instagram and Tik-Tok. Post a daily "live", people like seeing you "in real life".

- Hire a great VA to do the tasks that you are too busy to attend.
- As Papa G (Grant Cardone) advised; if you need to hire a cleaner/cook etc, do so. Pay them the $25 per hour to do the tasks that take you away for hours, do what it takes to succeed as an entrepreneur.

"You already know more than enough to succeed" - Elon Musk

As an Entrepreneur, I have witnessed more wishful thinking than "action". Action is key; big action = big results. Just keep moving; every day, move one step ahead, you will succeed.

Entrepreneurs must wake before sunrise and get in extra hours while others are sleeping, to get ahead of the pack This is a game-changer!

Visualise where you see your life going! I am on the road to being a billionaire. I play golf with Millionaires and Billionaires! Did I play golf before? Absolutely not! Change it up!

At Growth Conference, an event put on by Grant Cardone, I heard a speaker say "Go find a Restaurant where the In-Crowd go. Where the movers and shakers, the politicians and dealmakers eat; become a regular and sit at the best table. You never know who may walk in one day and demand that best table, it only takes one person to change the trajectory of your life."

Life as Entrepreneur is about constantly learning, reading, mastering skills that you thought you could not do. If one way does not work try another.

I remember, in my corporate job, I had to write Business Justifications, I told myself that I could never write them, they were too hard. But after writing over 10,000 of them; guess what! Now they are "easy"!

Something else I have learnt that is key as an entrepreneur; no one knows you better than you; you must become your own cheerleader. There will be many people who will try to shake your confidence, calling you crazy or insane for chasing your dreams. But no one knows where your journey will lead you next. It is your life and an entrepreneur's journey is a wonderful, exhilarating one.

Here are some key takeaways about being an entrepreneur:

Greatness: Who do you do business with? You need to surround yourself with great people. Build your community by including friends and the best people in the industry. Find spiritually-minded successful Millionaires and Billionaires who also live life in Source.

Responsibility is the price of greatness. As an entrepreneur, you must take responsibility for every facet of your business.

Mindset; As an entrepreneur, you need to focus on strategy and growth. Our thinking shapes our lives, we know that a person who thinks positively about themselves will do better than a person with negativity. An entrepreneur with a positive mindset can accomplish amazing things. Do not just demand positivity from your Team, demand it for yourself. Positivity and joy are essential for an entrepreneur. Even when the going gets tough, lead with positivity for yourself and your Team.

Passion: Passionate people are the source of real change in the world. As an entrepreneur, your passion will excite you and encourage devotion to your purpose/mission.

Beliefs: You need to believe; bigger, better, more significantly; and LEAD as an Entrepreneur. Do not buy into someone else's view of you. Too many people have succumbed to mediocrity, despite their enormous potential. Lead and believe.

Excellence: Perfect everything that you do, with granular attention, ensure you have a culture of Excellence for yourself as an Entrepreneur and your Team.

Impact: What impact do you want to create? Personally, professionally, and financially. Ask yourself what you are I am creating by changing people's lives? By leading them?

Courage: You must find your courage no matter what. If you choose to do something in life, do not be half-hearted. Attack everything with courage.

> *"To be the best, the only race you are racing with is yourself"* –
> David Goggins.

Source: Ensure you are harnessing Source energy every single day. Live where your life as an entrepreneur flows and where you recognise the subtle whispered messages that lead you to greatness.

You were born for Greatness!

Remember that!

Chapter Five

KARISHMA SHARMA

Keep your mind right

'I don't recognise that version of me' my client said, as we settled into our last call together. Tears rolled down her face as I read back to her what she had told me in her first session; anxiety, depression, misalignment, mental exhaustion, self-doubt, bad relationships, feeling lonely, not asking for help, feeling unworthy, her life wasn't her own, not standing up for herself.

90 days later and we were discussing her complete transformation. Feeling empowered, enlightened, staying calm and reflecting in situations rather than reacting, looking at scenarios from a new perspective, making time for herself, being the best version of herself and as a mother, handling obstacles like a boss lady and feeling so content. This is the power of having aligned clients - IT MEANS MAGIC!

Welcome to the adventure that is Entrepreneurship.

I was convinced if I started a business, it would be an overnight success. But I did not know or understand who I was, so how could I help others? To be honest, I was just looking to make some quick money easily. As a result, I ended up investing a lot of money in things that I did not need. At that point, I did not even know what my business was.

It was not until I did my inner work that it all started to unfold, and I really began to understand what my purpose was; who I was here to serve; and how. It took a while, but we got there in the end.

The best thing I ever did was find coaches and a community of like-minded people. I know it sounds cliché, but trust me; as you go through your journey, you will learn to appreciate that love, support, accountability, and friendship pretty much hold you together in your hardest times.

What hard times?

You tend to go through a breakdown before you have a breakthrough.

This is something I know well. At first, I kept thinking to myself, why does life hate me? Drama queen much! But when I began to understand that the Universe was testing me to see how much I wanted my business, it all became clear. The hard times were a necessary part of my growth.

There are 5 Up-levelling stages

The Wobble

This is stage 1. Where something hits you like a tonne of bricks and goes wrong in your business. You begin to panic and start to question everything. You head into a downward spiral.

The Anger

"GET PISSED" (as in angry not drunk), feel the emotions, and channel it all into writing in your journal. Rant about it and see what starts to come through. There will be some golden nuggets that you are probably unaware of.

The Light

Once you have got the anger out of your system, you start to feel relief and understand that you can get through this. You have your feet back on the ground, and you start to see light at the end of the tunnel.

The Clarity

Oh, I love this stage! Moments of understanding show you why you had this wobble in the first place. What is it trying to show you? Are you on the wrong path? Do you need to adjust something? Maybe you need to break everything down in the business and look at the cracks that need filling.

The AHA Moment

By far the best stage! This is where the breakthrough happens. You made it. Imagine that you just finished a Spartan race or Tough Mudder and you have received your medal. Catch your breath and look at what you have achieved. Now it is time to take action!

You do not have to do this alone. That is why you need a coach. We have struggled, tried, tested, failed, re-tried, re-tested and succeeded. We can show you the quickest way. You need to make sure you find the right person, the best fit for you. It is like a game of Tetris. A perfect match and you will be scoring points.

Investing in yourself and your business never stops. Get comfortable with this straight away. I remember the first time I invested in my personal development - it scared the hell out of me. I chose to feel the fear and do it anyway. I will always be proud of myself for doing that because it opened doors for me, helping me become comfortable investing in my growth and my business. I have spent considerable amounts of money on coaches and systems - but I know I would not be here today without having done so. Do not be afraid to invest in yourself and your business, it is worth it!

When I first started my business, I was adamant it would be easy, and I would have overnight success. In reality, I had failed launches and no clients; I constantly compared myself to the incredible women I was surrounded by; my niche was sketchy, and my energy was scattered. I had so many limiting beliefs triggering imposter syndrome; scarcity, fear of failure, fear of change, and a lack of self-belief. I was a perfectionist, never wanting to make a mistake and don't even get me started about my money mindset!

I questioned myself over and over about whether I was good enough to be a leader, an entrepreneur, a change maker, speaker, and author. Then it dawned on me; I was the creator of my reality and everything that was showing up in my life was exactly what was in my subconscious - block after block, limitation after limitation.

So how did I turn things around? I am about to break it down for you. Get comfortable, here are some golden nuggets for you.

10 powerful ways to be an Entrepreneurial Goddess

Inner work

First and foremost, I did my inner work. What does this mean?

It means dealing with the unhealed traumas and low vibrations within you.

I was pretty convinced I had neither. I learned that this meant dealing with situations, no matter how big or small, that caused a negative state of emotion - we all have these so there is no point trying to deny it.

Once I saw this, with the help of my coaches, I was able to reprogram my subconscious mind, remove energetic blocks, be high vibrational, focus on my positive psychology and let love conquer fear.

Reflect on where you need to do your inner work. Note: You will not see any significant shifts until you get to the root cause of your triggers.

Higher Self

Go inwards, rather than looking out to the world for answers and validation! Tune in with your higher self and your guides - who better to guide you through this journey than your non-physical team?

Spend time in the quantum field visualising and feeling into the Entrepreneurial experience that you want. Ideas will start to flow through when you meditate, journal, ask for signs and more. Synchronicities will begin to appear, and the Law of Attraction will work its magic - let go of the how. Just trust!

Listen to your soul

Feel, see, hear - what is it that your soul truly wants? What moves your soul and makes you feel good? This may conflict with what the human side of you is doing, but once you connect to, and build your business from this place, you will not only see results but you will be happy doing it, rather than feeling heavy energy (Never underestimate how important feeling good is).

Mastery

Doing my inner work helped me to identify my purpose:

'To help women leaders and entrepreneurs to break through their mind, body and soul blocks so that they can unleash a life and business of fun, freedom and feeling fabulous.'

I could see the rapid transformation that could come about from this process, and I discovered that I was pretty damn good at it! I knew I could help many people transform their lives, so I mastered how to do it.

What are you good at? Find your strengths and weaknesses, then master what you are good at and what you enjoy. Then you can then position yourself as the go-to expert rather than being scattered and trying to do everything.

Niche

Who is your ideal client? I hated this question but every coach asked me.

I was determined to help *everyone*. Despite being constantly advised that the more I niched down, the more success I would get. The reason I had so much resistance was because I did not know who my niche was. It was not until I started taking action that I got clarity.

35

You have to be certain and excited about your niche. Don't be afraid to test, trial and error, do whatever you have to do. If you're not 100% sure, then you are not going to be determined and you are less likely to get the results you want.

Moral of the story? - Do what works for you rather than others.

Love what you do - Alignment

There is nothing worse than waking up every day hating what you do. You have one life, so why waste it doing something that doesn't make your heart sing?

If you have a vision or goal for your business and the life you truly desire - go and get it. You may have to make some sacrifices, but it is worth it! When you love what you do, you are more likely to be in flow and alignment rather than constantly trying to force things.

Trust me; this is the place you want to come from because people feel the energy generated.

Money mindset

Your relationship with money will continuously be tested as an entrepreneur. It will require daily work. It is one of the biggest challenges I had, and I had to work hard to change it. It is one of the biggest blocks that I see with my clients too. The hack is to understand and embody the energy of money, abundance, prosperity, and the universal flow of giving and receiving.

Have fun and get creative

Never be afraid to try out new things. I never imagined myself as a speaker or best-selling author - it seemed like something only very successful people did.

But then I began testing things out. I started by going live on social media, speaking on a Podcast, as an expert guest, and before I knew it I was speaking at International Summits and co-authoring books. I realised that I really enjoyed all of this, but I had not factored it into my business originally.

Allowing that fun and creativity to flow through can help you come up with some epic ideas that will help you thrive as an entrepreneur. Don't allow that energy to get stagnant or blocked.

Your own routine

Find a routine that works for you;

- What time of the day are you more productive?
- What rituals do you enjoy?
- Do you want to start work early or late?
- How many clients do you want to work with?
- Do you want to work locally or internationally?
- How will you prioritise your health and wellbeing?

It is important that you choose a routine that works for you. Factor in your time off before you do anything else. Trust me you will need time out, and when you take it so much more will flow through you.

Keep your mind right

The journey of an entrepreneur is not a simple linear experience. There will be ups and downs, twists and turns. You may feel chewed up and spat out. Stay aware of your thoughts, habits, and patterns. BE AWARE OF COMPARISON!!!

This is a great time to shift your mindset and focus on the abundance in your life. Visualise what you truly desire. Stay resilient, reach out to your community, and focus on what is going right rather than what's wrong. Energise the good stuff!

Every entrepreneur's journey will bring challenges, but that is exactly what helped me to become the Entrepreneur that I wanted to be. Fear is just your subconscious trying to keep you safe. But staying in your comfort zone does not work if you want more.

Last but not least; remember to be yourself. You are uniquely you and you have magic to bring to this world. So bring your A-game. You've got this!

Chapter Six

MIRIAM HUSBY STENER

Living your WHY

> *'It's your responsibility to share your great work with the world.'* - Gabriel Bernstein

'Miriam, you are going to be something great when you are older.'

I do not remember who said it. But I do remember the words. And these words stuck with me for a very long time.

I heard the words as I was graduating from junior high school on the beautiful island Leka, in Norway, where I grew up.

It was a small school. There were 8 girls and 1 boy in my class, and I was graduating with the best results ever given to a student in that school.

Mathematics, science, religion, and history were my best subjects. Numbers were like music for me. I just 'got' them. They were easy and uncomplicated, unlike my inner world. Inside, I was battling anxiety, lack of self-worth and sadness. School was the arena where I was able to impress and shine.

After junior high school, we all had to move away from home to go to high school, since there were no high schools on the island.

Instead of choosing the subjects I was doing well in, my creative expression wanted to come out and play, and I ended up in a school that specialized in Music, Dance and Theatre.

Inside I had a secret dream of going to Hollywood and becoming an actor. That would be great, right?

High school knocked my 'being great' ego. I was battling with having been abused at 12 and 16 and was struggling, both with keeping all of this inside and learning to show emotions on stage. My drama teacher told me I was bad at showing my inner emotions and I created a belief that this meant I did not have a talent for acting. Another teacher had told me I would do very well in diplomacy, so I decided that would be my something great instead.

After finishing high school I went to study at the Nansen Humanistic Academy, in Lillehammer, Norway. Fridtjof Nansen† had been one of my idols since I was a child.

That year was a year with lots of red wine, exciting subjects like Ghandi's life and message and lots of philosophy. I also got to visit the Nansen Dialog centres on Balkan, where the Nansen dialogue centre had been working on keeping the peace for years. Celebrating my 20th birthday in the divided city Mitrovica in Kosovo, listening to all the stories, and seeing all the great work the centres did, I was beginning to believe that diplomacy was my 'being great' thing. But I was struggling with the anxiety of the abuse.

I went on to university for a bachelors in European Knowledge with German as a common language. Spent a semester in Germany and worked at the Norwegian consulate in Leipzig, partying with the guys from the Norwegian Embassy in Berlin. I was really feeling it. Helping people remain at peace or solving diplomatic issues, which would be something right?

Then life happened.

I was in Sweden, on a skiing trip with my classmates in the winter of 2006. On Afterski, walking around the ice-cold rooftop looking for someone who could give me a cigarette, I met my Gabriel and a year later I was living in Sweden.

After 6 months I got a job that really excited me. Customer services at Nordnet Bank, the leading pan-Nordic digital platform for savings and investments. High-class office environment and a fast tempo. I was in the corporate world! I was finally starting to achieve something great.

You know when you feel you have it all, and everything is looking so good from the outside? And you feel proud when you tell people what you do for a living?

That was me.

I became licensed as a financial advisor and I took on a role in charge of the bank's Norwegian corporate operations. I liked telling people I worked in the financial world.

When the financial crisis hit in 2008, I was working with customer services and had to deal with people who were losing all their savings. Some were heartbroken; some just stressed; some sad; and others some so angry they wanted to come to the office and shoot us all.

It was incredibly stressful, dealing with all those emotions, trying to balance them and give the best support possible to everyone, and my body reacted. I had such bad stomach pain, I even had to go to the hospital because of all the cramps.

But at least I was on my way to becoming something great, right?

Then in 2009, I became a mother to a little girl with beautiful blue eyes. We were surrounded by so much love.

I could not see myself doing anything other than being a mother. I enjoyed staying home with her until I became a mother again in 2011, the time to a beautiful baby boy with laughing eyes. But that birth brought me into postpartum depression with periods of darkness. The anxiety was back.

Life slowed down. My only purpose in life was taking care of my babies and our home. For the first time, I was able to reflect on what 'Being something great' meant.

Was I choosing jobs to impress others, so that they could admire me?

I realized I had shut down an important part of myself. The spiritual part.

I was not listening to my soul and hearing what it wanted to do.

I did not realize that I did not have to become something great, as we are all born great!

Doing something great is not about what others value as great, or about how things reflect from the outside. It is about what lights you from within!

What gets you excited, makes your eyes sparkle. And starts a fire burning in your heart?

I liked the financial world and my job at the office in Stockholm. But working a 40 hour week, plus 3 hours traveling every day – well I just could not do it. As a mother, I could not justify being away from my children for so long. This job was definitely NOT lighting me up from the inside.

What did I want to do with my life?

Being with my children gave me meaning. I had to find something that could match that feeling inside.

My search for a meaningful job began. Money could not be the main reason for me working. I needed a job that also felt that I was making an impact.

'Miriam, what happened to you? You were the No. 1 businesswoman?'

My childhood friend asked me after I told her about my recent discoveries in the spiritual world.

I discovered it was easy for me to connect to spirit and know the truth. I knew from childhood I had warm hands and now I could use them for healing.

I became a Reiki healer. Then, after experiencing the magic of an AuraTransformation, and feeling how my body was filled with an energy and a presence I had not felt in a long time, I decided to be an Auramediator.

I remembered my love for the four elements. How I used to dance them as a child and became a four-element profile partner, doing Body element activation workshops in Norway and Sweden.

I had started coming home to myself, but the people around me were questioning what I was doing!

I was listening to the voice inside that told me I was destined for something greater than myself. To know what this something greater was, I realized I had to stop seeking it in the approval of others. I had to listen within.

Fast forward to the summer of 2020.

During a meditation with my coach Dr Erin I was asked, 'What is the one thing, that if you accomplished it, would mean everything? Instantly I knew it was publishing books.

As a child, I was surrounded by books in my home. I read anything I could. My grandfather introduced me to the art of writing poems and in the darkness that followed me being abused and losing my beloved grandfather, I turned to writing poetry. Writing became my oxygen. My creative expression. The thing that revealed and released the anxiety.

As I changed, my poems changed. What did not change, was my passion for reading and writing. And my burning desire to become an author.

I realized what book I needed to publish first. It was also the one book I really did not want to publish. Exposing my inner world. My abuser was still alive and I was terrified of the thought of him even reading the poems.

You know when you have a strong WHY. A knowing that you have to do this, even though you have no clue how to? Well, that WHY was biting me in the ass. Telling me to step up and do the work needed to get this book out.

The book was already written, what was stopping me?

My limiting beliefs. And fear.

I had to clear out all of those beliefs and know the truth of who I am. I had to get myself to the point of feeling that it was safe doing this.

I happened to be in just the right community to do it, Soulciété. I had lots of amazing friends happy to assist me in doing my trauma work so that I could publish.

In March 2021 my book, 'Little Girl, Never More' was published on Amazon. A collection of transformative poems about being sexually abused as a child and taking your power back.

In July 2021 I had the pleasure of becoming a bestselling author with the book collaboration, 'Know your worth, goddess', one of the brilliant books from the Everyday Goddess Revolution.

I had finally realized what being something great really meant.

Being something great is not only what you do, but WHO you do it for!

When a lady in her seventies, a victim of abuse as a child, sends me a private message and tells me she can relate to the poems in the book. Or a mother tells me about the conversation she was able to have with her daughter, who had been abused because they both read my book, I know this is my WHY. Helping those being abused as children turn their trauma into triumph!

As an entrepreneur, you might think you have to do it all by yourself.

But for me, everything changed when I had a team of people supporting me on the journey. Thanks to people like my family, Leanne, Penny, Dr Erin, and my amazing friends, I dared to share my book with the world.

If you hear the tiniest voice calling you, you better start listening to what it is saying.

We all come to this earth as something great.

You do not need anyone's approval to feel what is already the truth.

Something great is your birthright.

You do not have to do *anything* to be great. When you start listening to that voice inside, that burning desire to do something, you will start doing work that feels great inside of you.

To be honest, there are days when I have to remind myself of my WHY.

Having a WHY is one of the things spiritual entrepreneurs have in common.

We have a higher purpose that drives us. A burning desire that is stronger than all the reasons we have NOT to do it. No matter how far we have travelled on our path of fulfilling our dreams, we KNOW.

And once you know, there is no unknowing it. You just have to do it!

If you have a burning desire, listen!

And as Gabby so eloquently said:

'It's your responsibility to share your great work with the world'.

† **Fridtjof Nansen**, (born October 10, 1861, Store-Frøen, near Kristiania [now Oslo], Norway—died May 13, 1930, Lysaker, near Oslo), Norwegian explorer, oceanographer, statesman, and humanitarian who led several expeditions to the Arctic (1888, 1893, 1895–96) and oceanographic expeditions in the North Atlantic (1900, 1910–14). For his relief work after World War I he was awarded the Nobel Prize for Peace (1922).

Chapter Seven

RACHEL WATSON

You are a gift

It often ends up that the thing we seek from others is the thing we need to give ourselves. Have you ever just wanted someone to look after you? Is there a chance that your inner child wanted you to look after her? Or maybe you want others to be more reliable, when really you need to be the one showing up reliably for yourself.

The things we fear work in the same way. We believe we fear the criticism of others when really it is our own inner monologue of criticism that hurts us. We hide away our gifts so that others cannot knock us down, but really the only 'who does she think she is' comes from within ourselves.

Maybe you have opened this chapter hoping to learn some neat and simple trick that will help you be more visible in your business and your life. Maybe you skipped it five times and are only coming back to it now because even the word *visibility* makes you want to gag a bit. Either way I invite you to stick with me even as I tell you there is no neat trick. The truth is much, much more joyful.

So what is visibility?

You are an entrepreneur who has given *so much* to what you do already. and you see that you want to give and do *so much* more. Your hard work and determination is outstanding, you want to make the world a better place, for you, for the people you love, for everyone! You have had the idea, made it into a business, thought about the website, branding, marketing, product, price point, ideal customer and so on and so on. The final (essential) cherry on top is making sure people know what you are doing and see you doing it. I'm going to say that again and put it in bold and capital letters:

PEOPLE NEED TO KNOW WHAT YOU ARE DOING AND SEE YOU DOING IT

And you need to know that it is safe to show up and show off. Which means taking a peek into that worried place inside of you and asking her what she is scared of and what she needs and then giving it to her. Because it is almost certainly something within that is holding you back. But I have great news; what is within you can be helped and healed by you.

Mirror, Mirror

Let's start by looking in the mirror. Yes; I want you to take the book with you and find a mirror if you can. The woman you see; just observe her. Judgemental thoughts may pop up or a feeling of discomfort. That is okay. Acknowledge those feelings and let them be. You do not need to shame yourself or berate yourself for having them. They are welcome here too. Keep looking.

Take five deep breaths with her; watch her chest rise and fall, see her mouth part as she sighs out the air. See her. Notice the shape of her face, the curve of her cheek, jaw, forehead. Observe texture, colour, marks. All welcome here. See her as a friend or lover standing before you. She would love you to compliment her. Compliment her. You know her worries and cares, what does she need you to tell her? Tell her.

Now place your hand on your heart, look into her eyes and say, 'I love you.' Say it out loud if you can. It might feel awkward or embarrassing; some feelings might bubble up. Every reaction is acceptable. Please do this again and again and again. You will find it becomes playful, joyful, and fun. One day you will glance in the mirror as you brush your teeth and with pure love and joy say, 'Hey sexy, I love you.'

Shine

Your light does not dim the light of others. It gives them permission to shine alongside you. That may sound a bit trite and there are quotes on pastel backgrounds all over Instagram saying much the same thing, but it is still true, so I am saying it too. So many women are waiting for *permission*. Someone to say it is okay to wear that, eat that, spend that, go there, do that. There is no magical permission granter sitting at a large desk with oversized rubber stamp in hand dispensing permission to those who deserve it. You deserve it. And if you still feel like you need permission, I officially grant it to you in my capacity as me, just because I said so, so there.

Shine your light whenever you can. Because stifling it hurts, because it is kindness to give others the opportunity to learn from you, because your light helps others shine, because your light makes the world a brighter place. There are practical reasons to shine too, and I do not want you to feel ANY shame about those. Shine to earn money, shine so your business grows.

In Person

Ooh yeah baby, let's talk about bodies! Shiny metaphorical lights and dazzling personalities are all well and good, but if you are not showing your actual self, your face, your body, your physical being then, my darling, that is your next step. And it is a juicy one.

Let's start by bringing your attention into your body right now. Take 5 more lovely, deep breaths and scan down your body. Notice any tension, any lightness, a place that feels good, a place that feels heavy. Scan down from the top of your head to the bottom of your feet. Just noticing and letting be. It is okay if there is pain; it is okay if there is excitement. Whatever you find, simply accept it as being there and continue the scan. Then, keeping your breath effortless and easy, turn your attention to your senses.

What can you hear? Birds or traffic, a telly in the distance or people talking outside. Can you smell anything? Food cooking nearby, perfume, flowers. Is there a taste in your mouth? Toothpaste perhaps, or whatever you last drank or ate?

Look around at what you see, this book, the room around you. Just observe without judgement, let it be. Now come back into your body and feel what you feel on your skin. The fabric of your clothes, the slight pressure of a waist band or collar, maybe there is a breeze touching your skin or warmth from a heater.

This body is a good body. This body is a good body. This body is a good body.

While you are feeling connected to your physical body I want you to send love and acceptance to it. No matter what it looks like or how you may have felt about it or treated it in the past, accept this body and send it love. You and your body are a team together.

Whether other people admire or dislike the way your body is does not change the fact that *you* can accept and send love to it. Praise does not elevate your worth. Criticism does not decrease your worth. As long as you accept yourself and send love, you will be okay.

So post pictures of yourself, have headshots taken, go to in person networking events. Let others see you doing what you do. It was never their criticism you were afraid of; it was always your own.

Visibility Vulnerability

What visibility means for each business will look different; there is no one-size-fits-all. For some it may be posting more regularly on social media; for another it is finally getting those photos taken; for some it may be submitting an article; contacting that person or attending that networking event. Whatever it means to be visible in your business, which is the thing you do.

But after you do it, you may experience the dreaded vulnerability hangover. You wrote the email/post/article and at the end sheer adrenaline made you hit 'send.' But the come down comes hard and your thoughts are spiralling out of control. Okay. That is all okay.

Firstly, you will get to the stage, if you are not there already, you can hit 'send' full of love and peace and there will be no crash – won't that be nice! Let's look at this vulnerability a little closer to see what is going on.

What you are actually dealing with is uncertainty, and your brain treats uncertainty as danger. A practise we do often in our house is worst-case-scenario. What is the WORST thing that could possibly happen because you shared your work publicly? Play it all the way to the end, and then check. Did you survive?

Now let's play the BEST thing that could happen. Play it until you are swimming in a pool filled with bank notes or president of the world. The truth is one is just as likely as the other. Now focus on what IS. You are safe, you are loving and loved.

The antidote to visibility vulnerability is self-esteem. You understand that you are a worthy human with a good heart who has experienced success and overcome challenges many, many times over.

Every other piece of advice has begun with 5 deep breaths, let's keep the trend going! Deep breaths are my panacea. Try writing down evidence that you are a worthy person. Give yourself time, you probably won't manage to come up with 20 in the first minute, that's okay. Let it percolate as you go about your day and write down any new evidence that pops into your brain later.

It's not About You

Great news! It's not actually about you. I don't mean that in an unkind way, I simply want to take the pressure off. Understanding that it was not about showing off myself was the best moment in my own journey into getting visible in my business. It is all about serving and helping others.

Isn't that beautiful?

Do not post to help yourself, post to help others. Get really, really, comfortable with the knowledge that there are lots of people in the world who want, really, *really* want the service or product you offer. It will make them happy; their lives will be better. It is not about you. It is about how much *you* can help *them*.

Chapter Seven

So go forward, dear one.

Remember to keep looking in the mirror; shine your light; love your body. Practising the belief that your worth is intrinsic; your fears can be soothed with action and love for self and that being a visible business is a gift.

You are a gift

Chapter Eight

TIERRA WOMACK MBA

Tame the Beast

Entrepreneurship is one of the most exciting adventures you can experience. There is something uniquely magical about the pursuit of our passions and when you set out to create your own business, you may envision entrepreneurship as being fun, fast-paced, and somewhat glamorous. I know I held this perspective when I first began my entrepreneurial journey 16 years ago. In many ways, it *can* be all of these things.

What is *not* often talked about, is the fact that being a successful entrepreneur is not without its challenges. You learn a lot along the way and definitely in retrospect along your business journey. For women, including myself, reaching success also meant many long, sleepless nights, overbooked schedules, new milestones to navigate, and unforeseen pivots.

As a female entrepreneur, you had this big dream, stepped out of your comfort zone, and built a business. Now your baby is hugely successful, to the point where you have hit your dream numbers. But now what? You are trading time for money - spending what feels like all of your time on tasks that are not growing your business. You may always feel overwhelmed. You cannot step back from the business. You are weary of hiring. Family functions are missed due to business obligations. The list goes on and on.

These are just some of the things we encounter during our entrepreneurial journey when we build a beast of a business. At this stage of success, it is normal to feel as though every challenge is a smack in the face, and you can find yourself feeling ashamed to have these feelings of overwhelm and disdain for your business.

You dreamt of this success - but now it doesn't feel good. Once you reach this mental state, it is not just about how to fix your present situation, but also how to tame the beast you have created so you can stop trading time for money.

I have seen it many times before with my clients, and I have experienced it myself too. It feels as though you've dug yourself into a big hole and you are not sure how to find your way out. When your business reaches this stage, it is draining and needs a little more special attention. These feelings are common; you are not the first, nor the last to encounter them. If you navigate this stage properly, effective changes are possible. It takes mental fortitude and courage, which may take some time to build, to incorporate these changes but once the process is underway, there is potential to see improvements rapidly. Every effort you make toward bettering your company, product, service, or expertise can help, even in incremental ways.

When I work with my clients running 6 & 7 figure businesses, we tend to focus on four key areas to help them reclaim their time and lives from their business. It's been an effective approach with my own successful companies as well. I am happy to share this approach with you, my fellow goddesses. You deserve to implement the next steps so you can start enjoying the success you've built!

Take It Easy

People think "automation" means cookie-cutter digital content and bots. But what it really means is anything that you can streamline, with or without technology. Start thinking about where and how you can make things easier for you and your business. There is software for just about everything - see where you can update or evolve your business systems and processes to do more with less.

Go With The Flow

Delegation is not always easy. Especially when you have built your business and brand around your incredible talent and expertise. It can feel impossible to scale or expand. But it is possible! The key is to approach delegation with a long play that starts *before* you run an ad on LinkedIn or any other platform to hire someone. When you do hire, how will you approach training them on your skills and service? What is your plan for after they are trained and on the job? Having the right systems and plans in place for before, during and after delegating duties to someone else will make your life so much easier!

Cut It Out

Businesses are a lot like nature. They are constantly evolving and changing. Expanding and contracting. Things that worked for years will suddenly not work anymore or need a makeover. Sometimes, this can include trimming things that are not efficient and clearing away any clutter or chaos. Most entrepreneurs spend too much time doing small, menial tasks and shuffling the business along when they need to be leveraging their employees and vendors to help. Even the most successful people fall into this time trap. Take a good look at your business brand across your entire company and along all of its channels. See where things are not working and decide what should be eliminated or changed. If your inner goddess is telling you it is time to cut something, do it!

Find and Follow Your Heart

You started your business because you loved the idea behind it. Or because it seemed like it could be a good market and concept in addition to the things that light you up, fueling success in your business. Remind yourself *why* you started the company at the overarching level. Look around. What aspects of it pop for you? Do you love to teach and lead? What about solving problems or building ideas? Find the big and little passions that your business fulfils. A fast track out of a rut is to reconnect with your passion in and about your company. It can be beneficial to your business growth, success, and your bottom line.

As I mentioned earlier, you want to work at preventing this lack of time freedom from happening again. Take a minute to think about when you felt the shift in your business happen.

- When did certain aspects start to feel overwhelming and impossible to complete in a timely manner?
- What stage was your company at during this time?
- Had you reached a certain level of success and if so, what was it and when?

Look for any trigger points you can find as you traceback. If you can learn what conditions may have set you on that course, you will be able to recognize these should they reoccur and handle them accordingly.

Good Change Can Happen At Any Stage

It is a whirlwind when you start your own business endeavor. There are a lot of different things you are doing at once, most of them for the first time. Ultimately, the decisions you make at every moment are what build your success or trigger setbacks.

Many of my clients reach the top and realize that they built the infrastructure their business needed on the fly as the business moved along. They may have had to compromise due to time, money, or lack of resources. That's why when many of us reach the top, it is a bit of a chaotic, cluttered mess. It's working, but not as well as it could which means it may be time to expand, scale or make other decisions. I know these changes can seem scary to implement.

The good news is there is always the opportunity for things to be changed. It might take time, effort, and investment, but it is usually *more* than worth it. Imagine having your time back, your rest *and* rejuvenation while seeing the potential for more success if you want. Let the desired outcome be your motivation and guide to finding what you can and want to do for your next big, beautiful stage.

Get An Early Start

If you are brand new to owning your own business and just starting out, you can use these practices and mindset right now, and bring them into your company as you build it. By setting the stage for the future business you want to own, you can improve your chances of reaching your vision with an element of freedom ingrained in your business model. That will be in the ethos of your business as it grows and evolves. The process is simple: look for where and how you can trim, streamline and power up your business & brand all the time. Put it in the mix of every decision and choice you make. This is how you have *real* time freedom.

If you aren't sure where and how to get started or what to do at every turn, just having the mindset and belief in your outcome can be good enough for now. Eventually, you will be able to make changes as you need.

Remember, Success Is Self-Care...

Success feels good, and it's supposed to. There isn't anything wrong with a goddess wanting and loving her own success. In fact, I believe you should! It is natural for your business to feel amazing and be terrifying all at once. Entrepreneurship - especially solo entrepreneurship, can be a roller coaster of experiences and emotions that change daily. It is also common to find that your business begins to take more out of you and your resources than it needs to.

Treat your business like it is a living, breathing thing and give it a good scrub down, freshen up, makeover or "spa day" every year or so. Do it right across the company; every process, every product or service. You can spend time on specific initiatives that you want to attack in the coming year. Or you can devote everything to one big effort that you know can transform your business.

Keep following the same process I shared above, any time that you find yourself getting sucked into a task that doesn't feel good, isn't driving your business forward, or where you feel you are struggling. It is a formula you can use over and over, but remember, self-care is a good thing...for you, your brand, *and* your business!

Teach It, Preach It

Start directing your business the way you want it to go right now. Even for those of you just getting started or in the early stages of your business, you can still fire up the mindset and belief that you are going to own your business - not the other way around, with your business owning you!

Take this exact same vibe into everything you do from today onwards. You are taking control of your company in an exciting new way and pushing it to a new and better level. Let it stoke the coals of the fire for you and everyone you work with. A good attitude and a good place to do business are contagious, and they can encourage others to want to get involved and play a part.

It's a *Lifestyle*

I can't say it enough. Being a goddess is a *lifestyle*. It includes your business, no matter how big or small it is, or when you started. It is lavish, orderly, efficient, and powerful. The goddess entrepreneur is the ultimate queen of her domain and world. Like any other incredible story, there might be times when you need to tame the beast. Your business will test your boundaries and push your limits. A goddess knows she was born to rule, and business and success are two of her favorite matches. Just like all goddesses, you have the power to reign in your business, *making more while working less*.

You deserve to live the lavish life you want to live and have the successful business you want to have, whether your vision of success is 9 figures or 5. It might be hundreds of stores and your name in lights. Or it might just be the red hot product or service that has cornered the market and you are staying local. There is no wrong vision for success. Just the one that belongs to you, and only you.

Tame the beast every day, in everything, goddess. Don't forget to bask in your wins and your successes while remembering that you deserve to have time freedom and balance in your business!

Chapter Nine

WENDY DIXON

Creating a New Life at any age

I had a dream, but I had buried it so deep that I had almost forgotten about it. I mean, who the hell did I think I was? How could I help other people? Who was I to set up my own business?

Perhaps you also have a dream but do not believe that you are worthy of achieving it, all too often we lack belief in ourselves, or we allow others to put us off achieving what we know is right for us; our destiny.

I left school at 16 and got a job, working for other people because I had no idea there was another option. Latterly, I worked for a couple of International Corporations. I thought I had made it, working for such world-changing companies. I marvelled that I was part of something so major.

But in truth, I did not fit in, the culture did not match my values, and although there were some lovely people there, many were just climbing the ladder, determined to fight their way to the top, often at the cost of other people's careers or reputations. I felt I was just a number, not a real person with a personality; it was a little like being a member of the Borg from Star Trek – no single individual truly existed within the Borg collective, they were all linked, connected, none of them had an individual or original thought; they acted as one mind.

I was often told how lucky I was, I had a fantastic marriage, a beautiful home, great holidays, a brilliant job. I knew that I was lucky but why was I still so discontented?

I had no sense of who I was anymore, I went to work and performed my Business Analyst job each day, this meant that I worked with lots of other people, and I began to realise that not very many of them were happy in their jobs either. Everybody complained constantly but did nothing about it, moaning about their job, managers, and colleagues. Of course, this just made me more unhappy, and I wondered if I would ever be content in a job.

When I was fifty-eight, I began to think about what I really wanted to do. Talk about leaving things until later! I had always had an interest in various aspects of spirituality; I had a knowing that life was not just about what we could see around us and that there was so much more to discover than any of us realise. My soul was crying out for more; if only I could uncover this and make a job out of it then life would make much more sense. Of course, the answer was always there, I always knew, and all of those answers were within, I just needed to learn how to listen.

My spiritual aspect is a major part of who I am, and I worked to develop this further, cultivating and learning more. Expanding my link with the Spiritual realms, listening to the wisdom and intuition within, learning more about Spiritual Law, Healing, Philosophy, Consciousness, Metaphysics, Shamanism, and lots more.

I loved working in this way but really had to keep it hidden in the workplace, I felt it would not be accepted in the corporate world and to some extent, I would be ridiculed because of my beliefs, I had seen it happen with other people and was not prepared to take that risk. I felt like I was living two lives, there had to be a way to earn a living and live my own truth.

So, after years of building my career, gaining lots of experience and qualifications, being employed in some fantastic jobs, I recognised that I had lost all passion for the work that I did. In the past, I had happily worked long hours and weekends and loved it. But now I was dragging myself into the office day after day, I had no interest in the work, the days became longer and longer, so boring, every day the same monotony. Even the journey to work became an ordeal, becoming worse every day due to road works, accidents, and the sheer volume of traffic.

I started searching for something more meaningful, Intuitively I knew it was time for a major change. After some discussion with my husband, we moved two hundred miles back to our hometown. It all happened so quickly, but everything slotted into place neatly, which helped confirm that it was the right thing to do. My husband found a new job, but I still had no idea what I was going to do. The one thing I knew beyond doubt was that whatever I did, it would be meaningful and would utilise my spiritual gifts; they had been hidden for long enough!!

I had worked for other people for years, helping them to live their dreams, build their businesses and live the life they wanted. Now was my time, time for me to make a difference, to make *my* dreams come true.

After we moved, I made the decision, that I would start up my own spiritual business called Intuitive Life with Wendy Dixon, I had a sudden realisation of my life purpose and knew what was important for me and my future. My family and friends thought I was crazy, after all, I was 59,! Wasn't I thinking about retirement? The simple answer was no, I was not ready to give up and retire. To be honest, why should I, just because I was a certain age? To me, age is of no importance and I love working with others to help them to achieve their dreams, no matter what their age!

One thing I did have was years of business experience. I had worked for many different types of organisations, from a small one-man-band right through to large corporates and many sizes of businesses in between. This meant that I understood how businesses are run. I had been involved in many amazing projects, including one where I was responsible for implementing a coaching programme for 250 + staff, ensuring each staff member received coaching to help improve their performance and reach their own goals as well as organisational targets. It was a great triumph, and the results were amazing for the individuals and the organisation. Over the last 25 years, I have continued to coach people helping them to achieve success. I knew I would include this in my business.

Once I decided to start my own business, I needed to ensure I had some income whilst I got the business running, so I took on a part-time job. This gave me the freedom to spend time developing my programmes and setting up the basics.

I started by defining my product range, identifying what I could include in my spiritual business, working out how to reach my audience. I set up my Intuitive Life Business account on Facebook, Instagram, Twitter and LinkedIn. From there I began linking up with lots of people online. I am pleased to say that my online connections started to grow.

I set up a couple of Facebook groups, Let's get Spiritual for all the "Woo woo" stuff and Embracing Midlife to support women in identifying how they can achieve their purpose and make the best of their life at any age.

I also needed to grow my face-to-face network. Although we had moved to our hometown, I had been away for 30 years, and nobody knew me. To get my name out there, I offered my services to spiritual churches and travelled around the Northeast working at different churches and networking with lots of new people.

I had always done readings, but I had no premises and did not want the responsibility or expense of renting anywhere. I connected with a couple of holistic businesses and was able to rent rooms as and when required. I also ran groups for psychic and spiritual development, meditation and regular workshops covering several subjects. Everything was starting to fall into place.

People started approaching me asking to join my groups and were requesting readings, healing, and meditation groups. I took on some bookings to do talks and demonstrations, and then …Covid hit and everything closed. I

It would have been easy to be negative, but I decided that it was important to see this as an opportunity to work differently.

Initially, I started attending other groups online but quite quickly decided to take the plunge myself. I ran several groups online, started doing readings online and it worked beautifully! I invested in a Zoom account and very quickly had people wanting to join my groups, In the beginning, I was a little concerned about how it would work, but it was amazing; a completely new way of working.

The groups continue to be highly successful and although I look forward to working with people face to face again, I will continue to work online as well. Distance is no longer an issue and I have people from all around the world linking up and working with me.

I had worked with many people in business as a coach. I knew this was an effective way of supporting people to achieve what they want in their lives. I also knew that many people were feeling lost, and were struggling through a worldwide pandemic. People were searching for meaning and understanding. As part of my coaching programme, I knew I needed to incorporate more of the spiritual aspect; helping individuals to grow their own spiritual practice and understand their life purpose; as well as supporting those who want to set up their own spiritual business.

Difficult times prompt people to start to search for meaning. Perhaps they experience a 'dark night of the soul' moment when they realise their life feels purposeless. This is often when we recognise we are not living our truth.

Ralph Waldo Emerson said

> 'To be yourself in a world that is constantly trying to make you something else, is the greatest accomplishment'

But it is possible for all of us to live a life of joy and passion; living the soul journey that we are here to experience.

As I reflect, I realise that there were many reasons that I did not make the changes sooner. I had lots of self-limiting beliefs; I did not feel I was good enough; I spent too much time listening to others looking for acceptance and approval.

Once I woke up to the fact that I needed to make changes, there was no turning back. I started work on myself, recognising that I AM ENOUGH and always have been. I no longer seek, or need approval from others. I recently read an anonymous quote that said

'You are the artist of your life, don't give the paintbrush to someone else.'

Listening to your inner wisdom, the intuitive self, is so important and the answers you receive will be just right for you.

In her book Return to Love, Marianne Williamson states

> *'Our deepest fear is not that we are inadequate. Our deepest fear is that we are powerful beyond measure. It is our light, not our darkness that most frightens us.'*

Andy Andrew says,

> *'Life itself is a privilege. But to live life to the fullest - well that is a choice.'*

My Intuitive Business & Personal Readings and Coaching programme includes helping individuals to shine their light and live their best lives at any age. I also coach people who want to set up their own spiritual business.

Within my programme, I use my intuition and healing techniques to support people in identifying and breaking down difficulties and blockages so that they can live their own soul's purpose. I help them recognise that age is not a barrier to achieving the goals that serve the higher self.

So my friends, at age 60+ I declare that I am shining my beautiful light, and I am living my best and fullest life, anyone want to join me??

Chapter Ten

YOLANDI BOSHOFF

Your soul voice matters

I remember sitting sobbing, feeling like an utter failure. I had spent months working on this project, I knew it was amazing, it was an expression of who I was and how I wanted to work with my clients, but no one was signing up.

I spent so much time working with coaches, using all the templates and the buzzwords, trying to figure out my niche. But it was just not working. I was angry with myself; with them; and with the Universe for this failure.

I needed to understand what was happening here, and why.

Then my husband, seeing my utter despair and disappointment, asked me why I was not listening to myself more.

He wanted to understand why I kept on relying on all of these people, outside of me, to try and guide me, to show me how to do something that he thought I was really good at.

That made me stop and think.

Somewhere along the line, I had lost my self-confidence. I had stopped trusting my intuition and my inner guidance to help me along the way. I ignored all the power and wisdom that I held within me, and decided that someone else knew better than me.

I work with energy all the time and I was fully aware of how our energy attracts and repels energy outside of us.

My energy is what attracted my clients to me over the years. People liked my energy, my message, and the work that I did because of who I was as a person. Because of the energy that I put out there in the world.

You know when you walk into a room, you see a person and suddenly your body contracts and you feel uncomfortable? That is your energy repelling the energy of another. There is some reason why your energies cannot connect comfortably. I see it as if we are walking around with a giant ball of light around us, and our light bodies interact with that of other humans all the time. Sometimes it feels amazing and other times it feels yucky.

This is all normal and happens all the time, some people are meant to connect and others not, no judgement, it is just a fact.

So when I see a photo or video of someone or read something they have written my energy will either respond positively or negatively to that person. We are always reading each other's energy even if we are not consciously aware of it. Our body is always letting us know, we just need to start listening more.

What I was putting out into the world with that project was someone else's energy. It was not me speaking to my potential clients on that sales page. It was someone else's voice I put out there. There was nothing authentic about my sales copy. I literally copied and pasted the energy of another person and tried to make it mine.

I was freaked out by this thought. What I was putting out into the world was something completely inauthentic.

My work did not reflect my unique voice and energy. No wonder people did not want to sign up, they did not feel comfortable with what I was putting out there and they could sense it was not coming from my heart.

Didn't I know that the reason my clients chose to work with me was due to my energy and who I was as a person?

It did not matter if I had a fancy website with amazing graphics and curated content. They wanted me. My energy, My expertise, and My experience.

I thought about when I started my business; I had the worst website in the world, but still, the clients were coming in. Somehow they found me and booked with me. It was just me and my real self, showing up on those first website pages.

I was not trying to be someone or something I was not.

But as I became more successful, I thought that it was important to show up more professionally; more polished; shinier. Everyone was doing 5-day challenges, talking about their six-figure businesses and how easy it was to turn into an overnight success. And I was starting to doubt myself. I was doubting that business could genuinely be as easy as just working with clients, showing up and being myself. Surely that would be way too easy! Why else would there be so many people out there teaching all these methods of becoming successful? That was where my dance with inauthenticity began.

I got caught in the age-old trap of looking outside of myself. I was comparing myself with others and wanting to be more like this one and that one.

Meanwhile breaking myself down and eroding my confidence in who I really was.

I knew that my clients loved working with me, their feedback reflected that back to me every day, but the voice of doubt inside of me became bigger than my knowing. After the miserable failure of that launch, I knew something had to change.

I had to find my way back to who I was and what I knew I was good at.

I realised that my Soul was expressing herself through me every day. The energy that I bring and project into the world is my Soul energy. Some people will love it and others will find it scary and others will not like it at all. All of this is okay, I am not here to be liked by everyone and I will trigger people through the work I do and how I do it too.

More than anything else I know there is a group of people out there yearning to hear my authentic voice. They want to hear what I have to say and how I say it. They want to hear Yolandi speak; they do not want to hear me quoting a guru or famous person, they want to hear all of what I have to say. This is not me being arrogant, this is just how I see and feel the world.

I had the most beautiful comment from a lady this week, we are collaborating on a project, and she had read the book I recently wrote, 'The Starseed Sacred Circle'. She said that she could hear me speaking throughout the whole book, she knew it was my voice she was listening to. That made my heart so happy.

Your unique voice is so powerful.

When you tune into your Soul and discover who you really are, people can hear you in the copy you write, and feel you in the videos you put out. The world is craving real and raw right now. In a world where we are surrounded by so much fakeness, so many 6 figure business owners trying to boast their way to fame, people are starving for authenticity. Not #authentic but the real you, speaking from your Soul!

If I had to ask you now if you are speaking from your Soul when you speak to your people what would you say?

Yes? Or No?

If you said yes, then you are welcome to turn the page and read the next chapter; I salute you for showing up as your real self.

If you said no, then let's have a quick chat about some important points that I would love for you to consider.

I realised that what was valuable to my clients was my experience and everything I had learnt along the way, during my journey through life. Admittedly, my journey has been quite weird with a fair amount of woo-woo!

My story started with me living a corporate life but breaking free from those chains to become the person I knew I could be, and create a job that I loved.

What is your story? Where is your journey taking you? How did you get where you are today?

This matters!

When you are marketing yourself, people want to know about the ups and the downs. They want to know about the lessons you learnt and how you helped yourself to get to where you are today. See how you have conquered adversity. Every deep painful experience you have been through and how you healed from them, matters to them. There is always someone out there who will need your guidance and your wisdom. Otherwise, you would not be on this journey of entrepreneurship.

No other person can tell your story in the way you can. You can try and use the sales page formulas and the buzz words, but they will not reflect your real self.

You created your business for a reason; you serve the world in the way you do for a reason. So start telling me all about it; share with me why you are so passionate about selling me this solution that you found. Share the work that you do that makes you happy and excited.

I want to feel that when I see or hear you.

Your enthusiasm for what you are creating, selling, or sharing is what I want to see. Because if our energies match and I feel your energy then I will want to connect with you.

If you are afraid to share your voice, your message, and your work for fear of judgement, please take a moment and think about this:

When you started on this journey of entrepreneurship something deep inside of you chose to leap. Something was calling for you to share your work, your voice, and your passion. This was your Soul calling you. From that place deep inside of you that is always nudging you, wanting you to share, help and guide those around you.

You are here for a good reason; you have listened to your Soul and answered the call by starting something. The judgement that you are feeling is another way that your human self tries to stay safe; keeping you in the comfort zone of the mundane and in the space of security. This is normal and happens to all of us during a big journey like this. There will be fear, doubt and judgement around every corner.

Your job is to keep remembering that deep inside you have a purpose and a knowing. And it will not go away, I promise you. So keep listening to that little voice inside.

Working through our judgements one step at a time is very important. When I allow my judgement to stop me from showing up I am not honouring my Soul calling.

You are meant to do this.

Start by unravelling the judgement. If you are worried about what other people are saying about your work, what you do and share – then consider why this is so important to you. Why does it matter what they think? Do they genuinely care, or do you just think they do?

Over the years I have learnt that my fears are mostly my own. When I feared that my parents would freak out about me moving from corporate to my woo-woo work, it turned out to be completely untrue. They were in total acceptance of me starting this journey and now, years on, they are my biggest supporters. But back then I was petrified. Now I can see that it was all my fear. Remember, those closest to us are often our biggest allies.

If they are not then I urge you to look at why they choose to judge you. It is their journey and their truth, if it differs from yours then that is all okay.

We are all allowed to hold our own truth and not be 100% in agreement with each other about our truths. So take a step back and look objectively at the judgement you fear.

Sometimes all you need to do is speak from your Soul and the world will listen!

Chapter Eleven

MICHELLE MASLIN-TAYLOR

Healing yourself

Let me start by being completely transparent with you and admitting that this chapter was really hard for me to write. I have never known writers block like it. I have spent some time working through everything that was coming up for me, and why it was so hard to write. Waiting for inspiration to flow. It turns out that what I want to share with you in this chapter is exactly what I needed reminding of to get back in to flow.

If you are reading this book, chances are you either already have your own business or you want to. You are probably a soul-led woman on a mission; wanting to share healing and make a difference in other women's lives. Sound like you?

The world needs you right now. It needs us. The lightworkers, the changemakers, the women stepping in to their light, coming together in community, rebelling against the old standards of comparison and competition.

But here's the thing. What brought you to where you are now - wanting to share your gifts with the world will not sustain you and your business unless you practice what you preach.

What do I mean by that?

So many of the women I meet who are walking the spiritual entrepreneur path have been though some 'stuff'. (Haven't we all? We are human after all). Behind their passion for their business lies a deep seated pain that they worked through and overcame. Very often they found something to be so transformational in their own lives that they just had to share it with the world.

Me? Well I found yoga to be the gateway to my own healing and other rituals and holistic approaches. It changed my world and reset my path. Then one day I realised I needed to share it! I needed to become a teacher myself. I immediately stepped up and into action and my business was born. To empower women with holistic tools that they could use in their own lives.

There is nothing like doing something you love, helping people, and getting paid for it. It is nothing short of magical to feel aligned and on the right path.

But something happened along my journey. I got busier, teaching in more studios, and running between classes. I managed my own admin and expenses and everything else too, with no team behind me. I did not rest when I needed to rest, because if I did not teach the classes I did not get paid. I overbooked my schedule with yoga, coaching and healing clients, leaving no time for myself.

I felt tired. Not vibrant and full of health and vitality like the lifestyle I was selling. One day I realised that my own practices, the ones that I was so passionately sharing with others, had fallen away. There was no time. If I were on my yoga mat, it was to teach or plan. I was running between classes and not stopping to fuel myself with nutritious meals; my meditation practice had dwindled; and I could not remember the last time I had time to myself to just soak in a bath, go for a healing treatment for myself; or take a long walk by the water.

Speaking to friends with their own businesses I realised I was not alone. Women are natural givers and caretakers and when we channel that into a business that helps others it is really easy to let ourselves become so passionate about it that we forget to actually take care of ourselves.

How do we find that balance? And where is the sweet spot for growing your business? Helping others but still honouring your own body?

When I started my business I heard many times how important it was to be busy and see as many clients as possible. 'It is not a business unless it's making money, otherwise it's an expensive hobby'. But where do we draw the line?

What does success really mean to you?

Is it being booked solid? Bringing in those £10K months we all hear about?

I learned the hard way but now I believe that success in a soul-led business has to be about more than the figures, it needs to be about the feeling, about the why and about the continuing growth and healing.

Holistic success that honours mind, body and soul.

In yoga we consider the body to be made up of koshas, layers that cover our soul and true self. If we are seeking success with a soul based business, it makes sense to me that we need to honour our soul and work through the layers surrounding it.

By this wisdom, our outer layer or sheath would bring us to start with our body. How is your body feeling right now? Are you taking the time to check in with your physical body throughout each and every day?

As a yoga teacher, this should be something that I was aware of. But I forgot. It something that can easily lost in the business of running a business. I have made it a habit to stop at least 3 times a day to simply sit and notice.

Carving out just a few minutes a few times a day to really notice sensations can bring me back in to my body, help me take stock of what is going on and then use that information to delve a little deeper into the finer emotional states attached to those physical sensations.

Once we have taken stock of where our body is at, we can know what it needs in that moment. Whether that is movement, breathwork, nourishment, rest, or even if you are absolutely all good and want to carry on with the task at hand.

I can find myself immersed in work, sitting with my laptop for hours on end. We need to move and stretch and release tension in the body. It does not have to be a planned activity, just a few minutes to stretch or a quick walk around the block will do wanders.

Are you breathing? Okay I know that may sound silly, of course you are but are you mindfully breathing? Are you breathing all the way down to your belly? Taking stock of your body and breath will help you to just take those few minutes to bring back in the most basic of practices to care for your physical body.

Working through the layers of koshas, we find the energy body and mind and emotions. If we are in the business of soulful business and healing, we have likely done a fair bit of work around these areas for ourselves. Consider this your reminder to keep them in your vision of success and the road there.

It is so easy to find ourselves caught up in comparison, overwhelm and not-enoughness in the world of social media and marketing our business. Take time to nurture your mind, check in with emotions and remind yourself why you are here, doing what you are doing.

I cannot tell you the number of times I have felt frozen in imposter syndrome, comparing myself to the other coaches and yogi's on social media, feeling like a failure and a fraud. It took coming back to my own practices, affirmations, and journaling to remind myself that I came into this work as it was a calling; to be me and to share my gifts in my unique way to exactly the right people who will love me. You are here to be you and your way, nobody else can do that.

We start our businesses with a dream of changing lives and healing but please do not make the mistake I did. Do not lose sight of your own healing. Take care of your mind, it's kinda important!

Moving into the final koshas, the wisdom body and bliss body, I am always reminded of our inner wisdom. If you are in the soulful line of business, or feeling drawn to be then maybe you have experienced an intuitive hit, a niggling idea that you just cannot shift. That's intuition baby!

Our inner wisdom has guided us this far, but from my own experience, when I do not make time to care for my body; when I do not do the inner work; when I do not practice what I preach because I am too busy. That is when I lose my connection to my intuition. I feel lost and floundering, unable to make decisions or know the next step. Overwhelmed and undecided.

Breathe.

That wisdom has not gone anywhere, you just can't hear it right now.

Intuition makes being a goddess entrepreneur easy, we already know all the answers. We are divinely guided and even when it doesn't make logical sense to others we can trust we are being led to exactly where we need to be.

The times I have felt lost (and there have been many), the answer has always been the same. To reconnect with the practices I teach, to embody these practices. When I do that, the answers come.

Our dharma, or purpose, comes from deep in our soul and is the perfect weaving of all our experiences. Our pain, our healing, our natural gifts, all rolled into what we are drawn to do, in a way that only we can. It is beautiful and simple.

What does holistic success mean to me?

It means continuing to be lit up by my work and allowing myself to shift and evolve what I do as I feel drawn to.

It means carving out time for my own healing practices as well as teaching them to others and making them a priority in my schedule.

It means valuing my time and using it wisely, not over committing.

It means setting boundaries on my time and energy so that I have quality family time and rest time.

It means honouring where I am at.

It means feeling good and making intuitive decisions.

It feels like freedom and breath and joy and light.

What does success mean to you?

Chapter Twelve

TANJA STEPHANIE RUG

The beginning of an affair of the heart.

> *"Have the courage to follow your heart and intuition.*
> *They somehow already know what you truly want to become"*
> - Steve Jobs

My passion. The beginning of an affair of the heart

I still remember that moment very clearly. It is firmly etched in my heart, in a loving and memorable way, ensuring that I never forget it. I feel deep gratitude and recognize other moments like it.

I was in my early thirties, ok at my job, yet unsatisfied and unhappy. I was also a working mother of two little girls. In the middle of a stimulating conversation with my girlfriend, she suddenly became very quiet and a bit serious. "I think what I'm doing concerns you too!" she said, while vividly describing a further training as a coach she was going to do and how exciting, interesting, and inspiring it would be.

My heart began to beat uncontrollably. I listened to every word she said, soaked it up and within minutes I felt a clarity within me that I rarely had in my life at that time: I would train as a coach.

I did not have the resources, time, money, or the necessary self-confidence. But a voice inside me - my deep intuition, a force that had carried me through years of training and insecurities, ignited at that moment.

I believe that we all have a mission; a passion, a certain talent, and a soul-plan that we are gifted to accomplish to serve in this world. It takes courage to follow your heart and intuition and it will not always be easy. But one thing I promise, it will be worth it.

> *"Many people are passionate, but because of their limiting beliefs about who they are and what they can do, they never take actions that could make their dream a reality"*

> - Tony Robbins

Waiting for the perfect moment and the power of action

I wonder if overnight success really exists. I have never met a successful entrepreneur, who did not work hard, with high focus and loads of dedication on their career. But with "only" passion, nothing will move forward. Focus, consistency, and a deep belief in yourself, that leads you to take action are key to running a successful business.

Years ago, I had a meeting with a highly successful and happy businesswoman. There were changes going on within my business and I had an ugly feeling of fear of failure in my pocket. She somehow saw through me. "Tanja, just do it! Do not waste your time with doubts and fear. You know your job. If it does not work, try something new. Come on, you are a coach, you know what to do," she said.

Ouch! That truth hit me. My own fear of failure was stopping me from walking my path, taking the lead and the necessary steps into action, in order to have a successful and happy career.

I am not a regretful person, because I believe things happen or do not happen for good reason, but after almost 20 years of entrepreneur experience, there is a tiny bit of "I could have done this and that earlier" inside of me.

Growing though, I became friends with the part of me that wants to protect me from failure and I have discovered a bold new friend inside me, that kicks (ass) and says: "Go, girl go, take action! Stop waiting for the perfect time, your time is now! Start today, even if it is one tiny step and be aware and full of gratitude to yourself for each."

> *"Always go with the choice that scares you the most, because that's the one that is going to help you grow"*

> - Caroline Myss

Decision making – get to know yourself

How are you doing with making decisions?

Is it easy for you and you just go with your gut feeling?

Are you a "pros and cons" person who tries to figure out decisions logically?

Or are you taking forever to make the "right" choices? Or do you wait so long that life makes the choices for you?

Making decisions in your business is key to your success. Hesitation and unmade choices lead to you standing still, chaos, misunderstandings and missed opportunities.

Understanding how you behave when a decision needs to be made is critical. If you are easy with it, it is wise to ensure that you have something in place to ensure that you make no arbitrary decisions. Talk to a business partner or take a conscious moment to reflect, before making decisions.

If you have a hard time making decisions, set yourself a time limit; to make sure you are not wasting your resources or missing opportunities.

If personal development is important for you, go with the "uneasy" choice. Growth is almost guaranteed.

"If you have knowledge, let others light their candles in it"

- Margaret Fuller

Feedback versus feedforward

I support some of my clients to grow their own businesses. Often, they have doubts about becoming an entrepreneur linked to feedback they have received from friends and family. Feedback given by our surroundings or the people we love and care about is a healthy and important thing to consider and to grow.

But here comes the BUT!

It is important to somehow "sort out" the feedback we receive. For example, the feedback received from a mother, who cares dearly about you, who has been working for a company for 30 years and loves security and a steady income, will be very different from that from a friend who has been a successful entrepreneur for over 10 years. Someone who enjoys their freedom, but also works many hours.

Check out the intention and values of the people offering you feedback but balance your own values, beliefs, and goals before you take their advice 100% on board. It is 'only' feedback. Advisory and not compulsory.

To discover if the feedback is received is beneficial for you, ask yourself:

- Do you trust the person, and feel safe with them?
- Are they benevolent, offering constructive criticism?
- Is their competence and experience in different areas, so that you get different views and values?
- If the feedback hurts, is it a feed-forward? Which means, am I growing with it? Or is it just pulling me down and leaving me with more self-doubt?

Ask diverse people, with different backgrounds, life, culture, gender, age, and experience to guide you on your path and support your light.

Money is the opposite of the weather. Nobody talks about it, but everybody does something about it."

\- Rebecca Johnson

Taboo? Money and finances

Many women I have met will do anything possible to avoid talking about money or even mentioning it. As if it does not exist.

For years I struggled with being the financial caretaker in the family and building a business. I disliked the subject of money; "Not spiritual, not important, not enough, the issue will never change."

We not only inherit money from our families, we also inherit the associated positive or limiting beliefs. For example, "It's only money," "Money doesn't make you happy," "Money is evil," "No pain, no gain," "Being humble, means being good," "I am not worthy of making money."

I was so fed up with the constant worry about money that I got help. Diving into my limiting family patterns about money, cleaning up all my old beliefs and changing them into positives for me.

"Money is energy and something good," "I take opportunities," "I love doing good with my money," "I am financially free," "I fulfil my dreams."

I still have a lot to learn but talking about money is no longer taboo in my life.

Find your own affirmations and heal the patterns that are taking your positive attitude towards money and finances away. Not everyone grows up understanding finance. But it only becomes a problem if you do not get help from a professional. For example, the advice I received, to secure reserves as early as possible, was worth its weight in gold and got me through the pandemic.

> *There is a special place in hell for women who don't help other women."*

> - Madeleine Albright

Network and mentoring as a key

What is the secret of a good network?

Be a good networker yourself and be generous with your skills, support, and kindness. Be the person you want to have in your network. And take time and effort with it.

If you decide to learn skydiving you are not simply pushed out of the plane the first time. An instructor jumps in tandem with the student, instructing him or her, ensuring that he or she overcomes their fear and arrives safely on solid ground.

It is a similar story with a mentor; he or she accompanies you in your professional development journey, encourages and challenges you, supporting you as a person with his or her expertise, experience, and good advice.

Great mentors will help you to find orientation; address and solve problems and develop understanding and patience. They also make valuable networking contacts and can help you master difficult situations. They offer you development and growth and will help build your confidence.

Decide what you hope to get out of a mentor.

- Strategies for successful career planning?
- Or how to balance your life?

On your development path, your mentor will ask you many questions, including personal ones. This will build a relationship of trust. Try to find a mentor in your network or a specific mentor network online or in your area.

Bear in mind that a mentor does not have to think or be like you. Often, it is precisely in the difference that a new, helpful perspective lies.

Do not set out alone; look for supporters. Friends, family, former colleagues, or bosses will all support you in rediscovering your potential. They know you and your qualities and can help with your restart by offering new inputs with their unclouded assessment.

Confidence and patience

As an entrepreneur, you can be independent, become who you desire to be and be a gift to others. But our subconscious mind knows, it is a long way to go and it takes a lot of blood and sweat to get there. It needs dedication and patience.

Keep this in your mind and heart:

- Do not ever give up before you see results in your business
- Plan the steps with the help of friends and professionals (business plan, financials, product/service, ideal client)
- It is ok to start a business on the side to secure your income.
- Take risks that suit your personal situation
- Let go of things that will not or do not work
- Keep the balance between being patient and realizing something is not working
- Watch your mindset: Is it fixed or is it growing?
- Take breaks. As an entrepreneur, there is always work to do. Take breaks to recover, when necessary. To become quiet in your mind and able to focus again
- Have a crowd around you that cheers and motivates you when you are down or feeling as though you have failed.

"The main requirement for spiritual growth: A yearning to know who you really are"

- Adyashanti

Chapter Twelve

Spirituality – am I all alone with this?

Often, I asked myself: "Am I on track, is this the right path for me?"

I was even upset with God, "Why are things not working, if I am supposed to do this?"

The people I was surrounded by were a reflection of my inner state.

"Why are you giving up your secure career?" or "Do you really think you can make a living with coaching?" I heard, and I was scared to fail.

But I grew curious about myself. About what I could accomplish and overcome. I made a commitment to my business. It made me strong and the option of giving up faded away with each year.

I often sat down praying, pleading for help. Yet I realized that getting to know yourself, with the highs and the lows, learning to accept and deeply love yourself, and making good choices - no angel can take any of that away from you.

To this day, I work with the spiritual world in a natural way. For me to get close to my soul's purpose, my higher meaning and to achieve professional fulfilment, I needed to take the steps myself. It was my soul's job to do and I was never alone.

The fullness of your yearning shapes your future. Your efforts will neither go unnoticed nor be far from a positive impact. Just trust it: the Universe gets back to you.

Chapter Thirteen

RACHEL SMITHBONE

Your business as your Sacred Offering.

What do you think of when you think about 'Business' and 'Entrepreneurship'?

I bet you don't think about a deep love affair with spirituality and service, do you?

But for me, that is exactly what it is. My business is a Sacred Offering. My work as a Conscious Entrepreneur models a different way of being in this world. A win-win of symbiotic, cosmic expansion where my soul's growth and personal abundance is directly linked to the magic I can facilitate for the community I am here to serve.

Humour me for a second... I want you to imagine we are at a party, and in this fantasy, neither of us are introverts or socially anxious (that last bit is for me and if it applies to you too, I FEEL YOU!) OK, we meet over a cool-ass beverage (mine's an espresso martini thanks) and we get chatting. We hit it off straight away, laughing and enjoying the vibes. It comes to the point where we find out what we both do for a living...code for me finding out whether you are working for the bucks or in love with how you spend your days.

You see, I LOVE hearing what people do for a living; whether they are spending their time doing things that light up their soul, or if they are working for the weekends. Whether they have a secret desire for a different life or if the weekly grind is fine and dandy, thanks very much.

As you respond (in this fantasy party setting) how does it make you feel? Has a teeny or a tremendous shame-shiver crept up your spine? A slight hot sweat perhaps? Did you shrink like the proverbial violet?

Or are you exploding with frothy excitement, a shaken champagne bottle ready to pop as you share your meaningful gains, your life's work, your soul's calling?

Maybe your response is more vanilla, right in the middle; a bit meh but not completely miserable?

When you ask *me* what I do, how does it feel to watch me rub my hands in glee as I share, 'I am a Conscious Entrepreneur'? Do you lean in closer to find out more or do you smile a little awkwardly, put down your mojito and make a swift exit?

My business has become my Sacred Offering to the world. It is an expression of my gifts, my talents, triumphs and joys and I love how it serves everyone I come into contact with.

What we do does not necessarily define us, but it does define how we spend a hell of a lot of our time. It defines the quality of our life; the extent to which we live life in alignment with who we really are; how we view ourselves; and how the world views us as well.

Even though I have run my own business for a long time now, I did not consider myself an 'entrepreneur,' the word was too loaded and I felt too small. Time to get curious and reach for my trusty Oxford English Dictionary.

> *'Entrepreneur' n. A person who sets up a business or businesses, taking on a greater than normal financial risk in order to do so.*

> *From French for 'Entreprendre' (enterprise)*

> *Enterprise (and this is a juicy one)*

Enterprise: n. A project or undertaking, especially a bold one.
Bold resourcefulness.

This kinda blew my mind! I have indeed set up a business and when I stop to reflect, I have indeed taken on greater than normal financial risks to do so. Not only that, but I am betting my family's future on my ability to create money doing work that sets my soul on fire - just writing that makes me sit up a little taller.

If that does not qualify as a bold undertaking, I don't know what does! And yes, I have had to be supremely resourceful to get this far.

When I was a child, we were poor. We were incredibly lucky to live on a stunning farm on the Exmoor National Park in Southwest England, but we did not own the farm. The threat of eviction hovered over us like a dark and brooding cloud. Debt was piled higher than the corn and there was no hope in sight.

My parents, brave and courageous souls, always believed that they could make life better for us. In the days before farmers began diversifying, they made a radical move; they set up a business. Already deep in debt, they borrowed more (back to our definition of entrepreneur; taking on greater than normal financial risks) and set up a business making sheep's milk ice-cream. I KNOW, COOL RIGHT! I grew up on an ice-cream farm!

I am so proud of and so grateful to my parents. They showed me what was possible if you dreamed big, thought outside of the box and were prepared to take a chance. They showed me how you could dig yourself out of a hole and create a life of freedom through enterprise. But I also witnessed the downside first-hand. Working every weekend, complete focus on the business, with no sense of security or normality.

But the seed of Entrepreneurship had been planted in me.

I knew I wanted to create life on MY terms. My core values were freedom and family, and I did not want to spend my whole life working for someone else, tied to a schedule that did not allow me the freedom to respond to the perfect sunny day with cocktails and capers. I knew that I would never be happy stuck in a cubicle.

I had always been a deeply spiritual being and dreamed of a life of freedom with time to pursue my spiritual passions. It did not seem possible. The internet had not yet blossomed into the wonderful mega beast that connects people from all over the world, allowing modern entrepreneurs to reach global audiences.

Fast forward to today and my entrepreneurial path has led me to this place; where I am able, with love and care, to intentionally weave together all the strands of my being and package them into a Sacred Offering that supports my fellow humans to live happier more spiritual lives.

I have endless debates with staunchly anti-capitalist people. They believe that 'enterprise' is a one size fits all behemoth of evil-doing. That in our increasingly binary world, there is no place for enterprise.

I strongly disagree with this.

I believe that 'conscious entrepreneurship' has the potential to offer a pathway for personal liberation as well as deep collective service. What do I mean by that?

OK, shit's gonna get Goddess powered real fast!

Let's start with the rather grandiose claim, that 'Conscious Entrepreneurship' could be your pathway to personal liberation. Like, seriously?

What if, that desire, that idea you have for a business linked to your life, your passion, beliefs, gifts and talents, is in fact, planted in you by the Universe? It is your unique way of supporting the world WHILST growing and expanding into your fullest potential? What if your business is your soul's Sacred Offering to the world?

What if all the experiences that make you uniquely qualified to have YOUR business, were the dots that you had to connect to be able to do that? What if everything in your life had perfectly prepared you to do the work your heart and soul are aching to do?

Trying to fit all that good stuff into the square hole of a role within government or another established institution and feeling fulfilled is as likely as plucking a rose quartz from your cabbage patch. When we work for other people, we often have to bend our natures to fit in with the company image, suppressing our individuality. This is not the energy of the Universe dancing with joy. This is an energy of compromise, restriction, and contraction.

In contrast, as a Conscious Entrepreneur, you are the bold, resourceful boss. The bold part is an expression of you being your magnificent self, JUST THE WAY THE UNIVERSE DESIGNED you to be. See where I am going with this? The resourceful part is your path of joy, challenge, and expansion. Exactly the reasons that your soul has picked this path this time around.

When you commit to spending your days creating a business that is your Sacred Offering to the world, a business that pours like nectar from your tender heart, you commit to a life of expansive, and at times particularly challenging, growth. With each passing month in business, you will continue to have to make bold moves, deepen into who you are and discover what you are really about in this lifetime.

You will grow to know, like and trust yourself in previously unimaginable ways. You will be forged in the furnace of your own vision and courage repeatedly as you have to level up. The more you level up and expand into the unique majesty of who you are, the more you will lean into it and trust it. So yes, I genuinely believe that 'Conscious Entrepreneurship' offers a pathway to personal liberation.

Now, onto the second part of my bold claim - that your life as a Conscious Entrepreneur represents one of deep collective service.

If you are still with me, you may agree that the life of a 'Conscious Entrepreneur' represents one of using your business as a Sacred Offering - the offering that you and you alone are uniquely positioned to share. This offering has its own vibrational field and frequency, its own destiny! This is a fancy goddess powered way of saying that it is meant to reach specific and particular people. Your business as your Sacred Offering means that it is Divine work, means that you are channelling energy greater than your small human self to birth something into the world.

When we create from that space, we are creating as the Universe and the Universe loves to use people to lift other people up! To create full-on, toe-tingling, win-win scenarios of such epic and unexpected proportions that our small selves could never conceive of them intentionally. When you are creating your business from that space, from the space of 'this is my soul's work, this is my sacred offering to the world,' then the Universe is using you to reach the people that need your exact medicine. Your medicine is here to heal and to support in a myriad of ways that you may not be able to imagine or are aware of. From subscription boxes to yoga classes and all things in between, the ripple of your Sacred Offering extends far beyond the people who directly interact with it.

As a conscious entrepreneur, you are bringing the light of your Divine Consciousness into every aspect of your business; from the places you invest and spend your money, to the ways you share on social media. You are in service to the collective unconscious as you expand, and you transform the lives of everyone you work with and encounter. You never know who you will inspire with your vibration, your work and your business as the ripples spread out across the world.

The life of a 'Conscious entrepreneur' is not for everyone, it may not be your soul's path this time around. It can be lonely; it can be hard and feel very unstable. It can push you to the edge of the cliff day after day, with the highest highs and the lowest lows, and no safety rope if you fall.

But it can also be the greatest journey of soul expansion. Creating with your own Divine Self, birthing original and authentic work that truly supports your fellow man in ways that are expansive, immersive, and creative. You could meet lifelong friends, facilitate life-changing transformations, and in untold ways improve the future for our species.

Think back to our party scenario, and ask yourself how you felt. If there was a twinge of longing, a frisson of excitement and desire, then it might be time to get bold, get clear and get resourceful. The life of the Conscious Entrepreneur could be calling you. It may be time to call upon the Universe to start co-creating your very own Sacred Offering.

About the authors

Ceryn Rowntree - Medium, Therapist and Guide

With a connection honed through over 15 years of conscious work with spirit backed up by a host of professional qualifications, I am about creating a safe and sacred space for you to connect with your own Soul and all of the power and wisdom it represents to help you live a life that feels truly aligned. www.cerynrowntree.com

FREE RESOURCE - Gathering the Collective meditation www.cerynrowntree.com/gathering-the-collective

Deanna Thomas - Acupuncturist & Wellbeing Mentor

www.deannathomastherapies.com

FREE RESOURCE - Marketing your Spiritual Business/://bit.ly/deannathomasmarketing

Iona Russell - Master Positive Psychology & Breakthrough Coach

International Speaker, Author, Radio host, Intuitive Spiritual healer, Co-owner of Hypnotherapy College and Creatix of The Soul Dancer Method to align with your Destiny.

https://www.ionarussell.com/

FREE RESOURCE - Soulful Business Boundaries / www.ionarussell.com/business-boundaries-freebie

Jasmin Baljak - Wealth, Success, Spiritual Coach to World Leaders

Jasmin Baljak is best -selling author, wealth, success and spiritual coach, businesswoman and entrepreneur to world leaders.

www.jasminbaljak.com

Karishma Sharma - Global Breakthrough Coach | Speaker | 2 X Best Selling Author

Karishma is a catalyst for Transformation, with her Quantum Results Activation System blending Subconscious Trauma Reprogramming, Spirituality, Positive Psychology and Energetics to help women succeed in business and life with lasting results.

www.karishma-sharma.com

FREE RESOURCE - From fear to freedom / www.karishma-sharma.com/ fear-to-freedom

Miriam Husby Stener - Author, Spiritual Psychology Psychology™ Coach, New Thought Spiritual Practitioner

Miram supports female entrepreneurs in finding their mission and purpose, creating from source and feel free to live their creative expression.

https://miriamstener.mykajabi.com

FR EE R ESOURCE - The ultimate Truth guide for conscious entrepreneurs/ https://miriamstener.mykajabi.com/ultimate-truth-guide

Rachel Watson - Photographer of hearts and souls

You are enchanting and Rachel's mission in life to for you to see just how amazing you are. Having photographs taken is a transformative experience and the images serve as an everlasting reminder of your beauty and bravery.

www.rachelshootsweet.com

FREE RESOURCE - Confident visibility video guide - use password "empowered" for access / www.rachelshootsweet.com/empowered

Tierra Womack MBA - Business Growth Specialist, Confidence & Wealth Coach

Tierra Womack MBA, multiple best-selling author, host of the Mind Your Business Radio Show, speaker & founder of The Brave Way, is a serial, multi-platform mompreneur of 17 years whose businesses have generated over 7-figures. As a Business Growth Specialist, Confidence & Wealth coach, Tierra helps female founders simplify success by combining mindset techniques and business systems to work less & earn more!

https://www.thebravewaytribe.com/

FREE RESOURCE - How to work one hour a day in your 7 figure business doing this one thing / https://bit.ly/Work1HourADay

Wendy Dixon - Intuitive Business & Personal Advisor and Life Coach

Wendy has worked as a Coach, Hypnotherapist, Healer & Medium for the last 25 years; she was awarded Yorkshire Prestige Spiritual Counsellor of the year 2020/21, and is a best selling author and Radio Presenter.
www.wendydixon.co.uk
FREE RESOURCE - Pessimistic to positivity guide / https://www.subscribepage. com/5-steps-to-move-you-from-pessimistic-opt-in

Yolandi Boshoff - Soul Coach

YOLANDI BOSHOFF is a Lightworker, Soul Coach, Author, Channel and Healer. She has guided clients from more than 35 countries to the re-membering of their Divine Souls again.
www.divinesoul.me
FREE RESOURCE - Soul Connection Meditation / https://bit.ly/yolandisoulconnection

Michelle Maslin-Taylor - Reiki-Infused Yoga Teacher and Coach

Michelle is a certified yoga teacher, reiki-master and coach who harnesses the power of ancient practices and yoga psychology, empowering women to take control of their mental and physical health with a personalised holistic toolkit.
www.michellemaslintaylor.com
FREE RESOURCE - Introduction to Chakras for self care / https://www. michellemaslintaylor.com/free-introduction-to-chakras-ebook

Tanja Stephanie Rug - Intuitive Coach, Trainer for Resilience & Yoga Teacher

Tanja Stephanie Rug, has been an intuitive coach and trainer for almost 20 years. She specializes in working with people in leadership positions in the areas of personal and spiritual development, resilience and self-love.
www.auxell-coaching.de
FREE RESOURCE - 1 x 20 minute discovery call / email T.Rug@auxell.de

Rachel Smithbone - The High Priestess of Sacred Self-love and Spiritual badassery

Rachel is the High Priestess of Sacred Self-love and Spiritual badassery on a mission to raise the collective consciousness by helping souls fall in love with their Divine selves through Sacred Self-love and Spiritual Badassery
www.rachelsmithbone.co.uk
FREE RESOURCE - The Energy of Enoughness Ceremonial Activation https://www.rachelsmithbone.co.uk/theenergyofenoughness